Parenting Is a Co

"A marvelous book that transcends the usual parenting advice and focuses on one-to-one relationships. Perfect for a new parent as well as anyone longing to reconnect with their child."

Stephen R. Covey • Author, *The 7 Habits of Highly Effective People* and *The Leader in Me*

"This is exactly the kind of book I wish I'd had when I was raising my two kids. Funny, isn't it, that parenting will be the most important thing we ever do, and remains the thing we're least trained for? Here, however, is the guide you want—full of truly useful information, advice, and, most of all, love. Simple concepts made easy by a double pro; that is, a woman who helps people for a living, and who's also a mother. Brava!"

Linda Ellerbee • Author of *Take Big Bites* and Executive Producer of *Nick News*

"One of the hardest parts about parenting is that it takes such a long time to know if you've done a good job. Parenting Is a Contact Sport is that valuable, wisdom-packed book that is always there for you as you navigate the challenges of parenthood. Having Joanne's expertise within reach is a gift you will treasure and a resource you will want to share with others."

SuEllen Fried • Founder of BullySafeUSA and Coauthor of *Bullies, Targets & Witnesses: Helping Children Break the Pain Chain*

"If you're a parent, read this book. If you're interested in creating powerful relationships, read this book. Joanne writes lucidly and honestly about all the pitfalls and joys of the greatest journey of all—raising happy, resourceful children. Joanne has been on this journey every day for over thirty years and has been a massive success. I know because I watched her daughters grow up."

Thomas Crum • Educator and Author of *The Magic of Conflict, Journey to the Center,* and *Three Deep Breaths*

"*Every now and then, a few wise people emerge with special compassion and competence for guiding us through the kinds of human challenges that test our ability to think, act, and even love. Joanne Stern is such a person. She generously and skillfully provides us with an approach to parenting that not only works but also creates a clear path that will open you to the powerful joy that is possible with parenting. It is readable, practical, and very human.*"

> **Jean McLendon, LCSW, LMFT** • President of The Virginia Satir Global Network; Psychotherapist, Trainer, and Consultant for nearly forty years

"*The unique connection between you and your child: Is there anything simultaneously so rewarding and challenging? Without jargon or scolding, this book shows you how to build and live a resilient and vibrant connection with your kids and stepkids. This approach is a bit miraculous in its clarity and simplicity, but Joanne Stern shows you that it can and does work. You will be the one they want to talk with—and listen to—now and for the rest of your life.*"

> **Joe Kelly** • Cofounder, Dads & Daughters and *New Moon* magazine and Author of *Dads and Daughters: How to Inspire, Understand, and Support Your Daughter When She Is Growing Up So Fast* and *The Pocket Idiot's Guide to Being a New Dad*

"*Our children today find themselves engrossed in a world of nonstop, sound-bite advertising, video game addiction, and relentless reality television bombardment. For many parents, it feels that we are becoming more and more disconnected from our kids. Never has the role of parenting been more challenging or more crucial. In* Parenting Is a *Contact* Sport *Dr. Joanne Stern masterfully and powerfully gives the wisdom and tools to transform our relationships with our kids as we build trust, honesty, dignity, and respect that will last a lifetime. This is not about controlling our children's spirits, but rather connecting with their hearts. This tremendous book will help you break through with your children and bring your family together as never before!*"

> **Brian Biro** • America's Breakthrough Coach and Author of seven books, including *Beyond Success: The 15 Secrets to Effective Leadership and Life!*

"I do not know of any parent who would not greatly benefit from Joanne's book. Any person who hopes to be an inspiration to children needs this information. I wish she had written it decades ago, but it's not too late to communicate with your children—no matter how old they are. This is a good place to start. Frankly, I wish my own parents had had this book when I was growing up. It's really fantastic!"

Susie Scott Krabacher • Founder of The Mercy and Sharing Foundation and Author of *Angels of a Lower Flight*

"Joanne Stern's book is beautiful, practical, and wise. Being both a parent and a therapist, she knows what parents need to know and what kinds of advice actually work. Her emphasis on connection—and how to connect—is spot-on. Her love of children and parents shines through on every page. This book will help everyone who reads it."

Edward Hallowell, M.D. • Author of *Driven to Distraction* and *The Childhood Roots of Adult Happiness,* and founder of The Hallowell Center for Cognition and Emotional Health

Parenting
IS A
Contact
Sport

**8 WAYS TO STAY CONNECTED
TO YOUR KIDS FOR LIFE**

Joanne Stern, PhD

GREENLEAF
BOOK GROUP PRESS

Published by Greenleaf Book Group Press
Austin, TX
www.greenleafbookgroup.com

Distributed by Greenleaf Book Group LLC

For ordering information or special discounts for bulk purchases, please contact Greenleaf Book Group LLC, PO Box 91869, Austin, TX 78709, (512) 891-6100.

Cover and interior design by Robert Mott for Robert Mott & Associates

Publisher's Cataloging-In-Publication Data
(Prepared by The Donohue Group, Inc.)

Stern, Joanne.
   Parenting is a contact sport : 8 ways to stay connected to your kids for life / Joanne Stern. — 1st ed.

   p. ; cm.

   ISBN-13: 978-1-929774-22-7
   ISBN-10: 1-929774-22-2

1. Parenting. 2. Parenting—Anecdotes. 3. Parent and child—Anecdotes. 4. Child rearing—Anecdotes. I. Title.

HQ755.85 .S84 2009
306.874   2008938174

Part of the Tree Neutral™ program, which offsets the number of trees consumed in the production and printing of this book by taking proactive steps, such as planting trees in direct proportion to the number of trees used: www.treeneutral.com

Printed in the United States of America on acid-free paper

09 10 11 12 13 14   10 9 8 7 6 5 4 3 2 1

First Edition

To Carol and Andrea

CONTENTS

by Linda Ellerbee

PARENTING MAY BE SIMPLE, but simple never was the same thing as easy. Raising a child is the hardest and most important job any of us will ever do—and the one for which most of us are the least prepared. I don't recall "Parenting 101" being offered to me in any school at any time. Nor did instructions come with my daughter or my son.

We survived, my children and I, but I could have been a much better mother to them. I know this now. I even knew it then. What I didn't know was *how* to be the parent I wanted to be. For one thing, I didn't understand that to raise a child you have to stop being one. My mistakes bled over all three of us.

I didn't know Joanne Stern back then either, so I didn't know it doesn't have to be that way.

And the book you're now holding in your hands didn't exist yet.

My loss.

But not yours.

Joanne Stern not only knows (and can explain) *how* she successfully raised her daughters—keeping connected with them while still staying one step ahead of them—she knows (and can explain) how you can do it too. Doesn't matter whether you're a mother or a father.

Whether you're single or partnered. Whether you're raising boys or girls or both. Whether it's one child or many. Joanne understands what you're going through—and what they're going through—and how you can all come through it unscarred, stronger, more loving—and cemented together in a relationship built to last.

Yes, Joanne Stern is my friend. She's also a psychotherapist, mother, and wise woman. She's a teacher. A leader. A giver of gifts to those of us who need them. And this too is important: What Joanne has to say makes sense.

It also works.

For the last eighteen years I've been lucky enough to spend my professional life—as producer, writer, and anchor of *Nick News*, the most watched children's news program in television history—listening to other people's children. The purpose of our series is to give children a voice: About divorce. Child abuse. Bullying. Popularity. Peer pressure. Drugs. Sex. The Internet. Friendship. Feeling different. *Being* different. Sickness. Death. Loss. About all the issues children and parents can face in an ever-more-complicated world.

I may not have been as good a parent as I wanted to be, but I'm a pretty good journalist, and after so many years of hearing hundreds if not thousands of kids speak their hearts and minds to me, a total stranger, on the tough issues, the ones that tripped me up so when I was raising my daughter and son, I can spot those children whose parents are getting it right.

Their kids stand out. They are caring, courageous, and confident. And open. It's not that nothing bad ever happens in theirs lives; it's that they're more prepared to deal with what may come. And they don't feel alone. They know—they really and truly *know*—that their parents (or parent) are on their side. No matter what. Even when the parent says no.

How those parents got so smart was still somewhat of a mystery to me until I read Joanne's book. She doesn't make you feel guilty because you're not the perfect parent. She understands that no parent is perfect. But she knows simple stuff (some of it is even easy, too) that you can do to ensure that the relationship you have with your children gets off on the right foot—and stays on that foot as much as is humanly possible. What's more, she believes that if it's broke, it *can* be fixed.

If I could do it all over again, I would. Too bad none of us ever gets a do-over when it comes to raising our kids. However, with this book, you can get to a new beginning, no matter how old your kids are, or how distant and strained your relationship with them might be. As Joanne says, it's never too late to start.

Or too early.

My children have sons and daughters of their own now. And I shall make sure my children have copies of this book. They are smarter than I am, my children, but they will still need the help Joanne can offer. Not just for their kids' sake, but for their own.

And for mine.

Because you never stop being a parent.

Not if you're lucky.

ACKNOWLEDGMENTS

I CAN'T IMAGINE HAVING WRITTEN THIS BOOK ALONE—without the encouragement, help, advice, and cheering from many friends and family members all along the way. Caring relationships really *do* matter in every endeavor and experience in life, and I am so very grateful to the many people who have contributed to this accomplishment in *my* life.

To Carol and Andrea for lending me your stories and for trusting that I would tell them with the dignity and respect we have shared throughout our lives together. You have enriched and enlarged my life more than you could ever know and have brought joy that lights up my world.

To my psychotherapy clients: I have felt privileged to work with you over the years and honored that you shared the very intimate and often painful issues of your lives with me. I have disguised your stories and changed your names to protect your confidentiality and anonymity. Help often goes in both directions, and I hope you know how much you have helped me to learn about life and love, pain and struggle, rebuilding and renewing.

To Carolyn Fields for being such a dear and long-standing friend. You stood by me from the beginning, read multiple drafts and revisions with careful attention, and voiced valuable critiques and contributions. You're the best, and I will always appreciate you.

To Linda Ellerbee for your friendship and helpful tips along the way. You have just hung in there with me, and it has meant everything to me to have your support. I value so much our continually growing bond.

To Deni Dietz for editing my early work. Thank you for making my manuscript presentable and for introducing me to the publishing world.

To James Kaiser, Brad Listi, Lowell Wightman, Brian Biro, Gail Holstein, Adrianne Ahren, Jennifer Leigh, and Cathy O'Connell for being so generous with your time and expertise about the book world. I thank you.

To Carol Myer, Burt Hixson, Gerry Battle, Harriet Gottlieb, Ruth Shuman, Janet Lapin, Nancy Hopper, Kenton Kuhn, Cathy Crum, Deborah Hansen, Steve Goldenberg, Andy Hecht, Jordan Rogers, Forrest Hale, Rob Seideman, Sigi Hale, and Diane Moore. You have all given to me in your own ways. Thank you for reading early versions, sharing your opinions and your knowledge, introducing me to people who could help me progress, and, most importantly, rooting for me.

To Joe Kelly for mentoring and coaching me all along the way. You helped me hone my thinking and sharpen my ability to articulate my concepts. I really needed someone to guide me through the maze, and I am so grateful that you were there for me.

To Jon and Sylvia (Gomez) Duncanson: Wow! You two are exceptional. Not only are you masters at making videos, but your sincere interest in my success is overwhelming. Your news background makes your suggestions, your ideas, and your help more precious to me than you could ever know. Thank you so much for your contributions and, even more, for your friendship.

To Karen Risch: You are extraordinary. It was comforting to turn over my work to you and trust you to make it better. You are truly gifted, not only as an editor but also as an advisor and consultant in publishing. Everyone should be so fortunate to have an editor who has become a friend.

To Robert Mott: You are the greatest graphic designer! Thank you for your expert and creative work. You've put up with my questions, my doubts, my confusion, and my fumbling, and handled my project so well—sometimes in spite of me! I appreciate you so much.

To all the people at Greenleaf Book Group for making my book a reality. My special thanks to Justin Branch, Bill Crawford, Erin Nelsen, Matt Donnelley, Lari Bishop, Alan Grimes, and Ryan Wheeler for being so responsive and so professional.

From the bottom of my heart I give my love and my thanks to my family. You are my greatest blessings.

To Carol Stern for pouring out your loving and compassionate heart to me. You read, critiqued, edited, and gave me your thoughts. But most of all, you helped me to believe in myself. You are a treasure to me.

To Andrea Himoff for getting me started and keeping me going. I can't believe how much of your time, your skills, and your caring you gave to me. You helped me to think and to rewrite, and you never stopped encouraging me. I couldn't have done it without you.

To Adam Himoff for your writing talent, your wisdom, and your deep and thoughtful comments. You have an amazing ability to say hard things in the most gentle and persuasive way. I value you, not only with my manuscript, but in my life.

To Terry Hale, my husband and constant supporter, for walking side by side with me. You have an over-the-top ability to think extemporaneously about my ideas and articulate them better than I ever could. I appreciate you so much—for nurturing my heart and for being the best partner I could ever have.

PARENTING MY TWO DAUGHTERS has been the greatest challenge and the greatest reward of my life. Not only was I supposed to put out the fires, shore up the cracks, and fill in the potholes in Carol's and Andrea's lives, but I was expected to do it with calm reason, profound wisdom, and deep understanding. It was my responsibility to teach them; to guide and counsel them; and to model appropriate values, ethics, and behaviors—all while living my own life, which was filled with its own crises and chaos.

Kids of all ages deserve to have good parents. Of course! But how do you be a good parent, day in and day out? Some days are smooth, easy, and blissful. Others knock the wind right out of you. Not that I wish any of this on you, but . . .

What would you do if your sixteen-year-old fell down drunk at a party and broke her nose on the keg? Or if your fourteen-year-old announced she was ready to have sex with her boyfriend?

How would you deal with your adolescent son being rude and insolent to you, accusing you and blaming you for everything that's wrong in his life? Or your six-year-old getting suspended from school for his bad behavior?

Suppose your twelve-year-old started sneaking out of the house, hitchhiking to the center of town to hang out with kids ten years older. How would you handle that?

What if your eighteen-year-old returned home from studying abroad and blurted out that she was pregnant and a guy she'd met in a bar was her baby's daddy?

I'm not asking what you would do two weeks later, after you'd had time to read a couple of books, think about it, see a therapist, or talk with some friends. I mean right there on the spot, because that's when you'd have to make your first response. That's when you'd either make it or break it with your children, because that's when they'd learn whether you're open and compassionate or judgmental and critical. That's when your kids would decide whether to trust you with their difficult stuff.

In my psychotherapy practice, I have counseled troubled, confused, and disgruntled parents who were working their way through the wide range of problems, calamities, and explosions that every family experiences. They've wanted to know how to discipline rebellious teenagers, how to help younger children get organized, and how to create a friendlier environment in the home. They've needed help in learning how to talk with their kids about painful issues like divorce and death in the family. When I taught parenting courses, people often asked me how to get their children to make their beds, excel in school, and participate eagerly in family activities. They were concerned about their kids getting involved in drugs and alcohol and hanging out with the wrong crowd. They wanted the inside track on how to teach their kids responsibility, honesty, and ambition and how to help them set boundaries and make good decisions about their future.

They were concerned about the same things you are.

As a mom myself, I've been deeply interested in all of these issues for my daughters, too. Our lives weren't always trouble free; their father and I divorced when they were little, and we took years to deal with that event and its causes. There were plenty of other bumps in the road, too. Certainly, as I was wading through my own maze of parenthood, there were times when I needed help. Maybe a small bolt of lightning to knock a brilliant idea into my head. Or a calm voice to whisper the right answer in my ear. Seldom did anything ever come to me from the outside at the moment of need. I had to rely on myself, just as you have to rely on yourself.

During those times, I relied on my own basic underlying principle for raising my kids. When they were young, I'd decided to build a strong, trusting relationship to guide me through everything I did with them, a relationship that would give me real contact with them. Not just hugging them, but spending time with them, doing activities with them, and most of all, talking with them. I began to think that effective parenting is all about sticking close and staying connected.

It's a *contact* sport.

What a simple concept. Not a lot of how-to steps to remember, because in the middle of a big emotional issue, it's hard to remember a long list of things you're supposed to do. Remembering and focusing on one thing—the relationship—was much simpler.

Early on, I realized my daughters would talk to *someone*. Who would it be? A kid who was as young, immature, and inexperienced as they were? One who watched MTV all day or was jealous and didn't want them to succeed? A kid who got his or her information from the exaggerated, distorted media? Or one who abused drugs and alcohol? Aren't these the kids who exert the dreaded peer pressure we parents talk about and worry over?

Peers influence our children, in great part, because other kids *listen*, they *become engaged*, and they're *interested* in what their friends say and do. If we want to counterbalance this influence, then *we* need to be the ones who listen, become engaged, and show interest in what our children say and do. We need to learn to create a more positive and beneficial relationship with them than the bonds they share with their peers. We need relationships that are supportive, encouraging, and compassionate, and we need to maintain contact that is both meaningful and helpful so our children will choose to talk with us instead.

Like you, I wanted to be the person my children talked to—and listened to. I wanted to have the opportunity to influence them, mentor them, and coach them, so I tried to create and maintain a safe haven for them, a place they could turn to and feel assured that they would not be judged, criticized, or put down. I tried to treat them with dignity and respect, the same way I expected to be treated by them.

The result? We developed a deep friendship. Not like the often temporary or volatile relationships they had with kids their own ages. Not a friendship in which competition, betrayal, or abandonment could seep in. Since our roles were clear and distinct, we didn't operate as peers with equal privileges or responsibilities. We shared openly but appropriately, because our friendship had boundaries. It was defined by my commitment to their well-being. Because they knew I had their best interests at heart, our bond of friendship remained steadfast even in the midst of tumult.

I wasn't always successful, no matter how much I wanted to be. I blew it many times, sometimes unintentionally and sometimes because I was too self-absorbed or busy to think about their best interests. On occasion I was simply at a loss—I missed the mark and chose the wrong direction—but we always had our relationship. During the good times we had even more fun because we enjoyed being together. During the gritty times, in the midst of pain and tears, we relied on our relationship to talk through problems, get the support we needed, and make it to the other side.

Over time, I came to understand that effective parenting depended entirely upon me developing a solid relationship with my daughters, and I discovered that being the best parent I could be was the optimal way to help my daughters be the best they could be—to fulfill their dreams and to reach their own potentials.

This principle of building a relationship helped me through the labyrinth of my own parenting, and it's the principle I relied upon with distressed parents who came to me for family counseling. It's also the bedrock upon which I've grounded the parenting courses I've taught. As I said, the concept is simple: When a problem arises, don't panic. Don't react. *First, secure the relationship.* Make sure you don't damage your connection with your kids. Maintain and even increase your contact. There's plenty of time to solve the problem after they know you understand, you care, and you're on their side.

Of course, child rearing isn't always easy. It may constitute the most difficult activity you'll undertake in your entire life. It's not something to approach casually or without the necessary information. Many young couples long to get pregnant; they yearn to have a baby, but many don't think much beyond that. (You don't hear many people say they can't wait to have a nine-year-old or a teenager, do you?) So they read books and talk to their doctors about how to have a healthy pregnancy and an uncomplicated birth. They learn how to care for an infant, and they read about how that infant will grow and develop into a toddler. Then they stop reading and learning and begin to wing it.

Learning about children—their behaviors, needs, desires, and feelings, as well as how they grow, develop, and interact with others—continues to be an important part of parenting, certainly far beyond the toddler years. Kudos to you for continuing your education with this book!

Among the many questions clients have asked me, two seem most common. First, "What do I do if I don't already have a good relationship with my child?" You can begin building or rebuilding trust, respect, and love right now. Back up, rewind, start again. This can be hard, but you knew parenting wouldn't always be a breeze, right? This book can help you reconnect with your child, no matter how distant you may have become.

The other frequent question is about when it will be over: "When does parenting end?" In my experience as a therapist and a mom, parenting never ends. That gives us every reason to wipe the tears, heal the wounds, and rebuild the broken bridges. Parent–child relationships last a lifetime. Why not do everything we can to make them the most beautiful friendships in our lives?

A couple of years ago I decided to write about my experiences for Carol and Andrea, now that they're grown. I wanted to tell them again what I had learned about building strong relationships with them when they were kids. I hoped to help prepare them for the day when they, too, would be parents. I began to make notes, recalling the stories that would illustrate my points.

I realized that what came up in my family was probably not much different from what comes up in most families. We parents have so much in common, regardless of our individual circumstances or lifestyles, because we're all dealing with similar issues with our kids. Deep down inside, we're all pretty much the same. I decided to share my journey as a mom and a therapist with you and others like you, who care deeply about building a lifetime of connection with a child. I decided to include many of my daughters' stories, told with blunt honesty. I've written these stories to give you the most vivid pictures of our reality.

Of course, the stories I share in this book aren't scripts. I'm not attempting to dictate your family's morals or your decisions, nor do I have an agenda of making you more permissive or restrictive in your parenting choices. Please take these for what they are: my family stories, based on our unique personal history and personalities, which illustrate essential *principles* for staying connected. Since I know our goal is the same—a trusting, intimate relationship with our children that lasts for the rest of our lives—I can share the details of my interactions with my daughters with faith that you'll see them as I intend: an unshaded window into real-life parenting rooted in the parent–child relationship.

This book has a central theme and theory of the power of the relationship, but it's focused on the realities of parenting—deeply personal examples from my own life, as well as situations brought to me by my clients during my twenty years of practicing psychotherapy. (I've changed their names and disguised details to protect their anonymity.) Our dilemmas, our struggles, and our pain are indeed more alike than different.

Some people have asked if Carol and Andrea know I've written these intimate details about them. Yes. We're friends, and I hardly do anything they don't know about. Not only do they know about the stories, but they also helped me remember some of them and suggested adding them to the book. I invite you to read their responses to this book in the afterword.

Because most families face similar situations and problems, I'm hoping my stories will resonate with you and help put you in touch with the experiences and feelings of your daily life in your own family. My ultimate desire is that, whether you already have kids or are about to have kids, whether you are a stepparent in a blended family or didn't have a good relationship with your own parents, these stories will stimulate your thinking about families and give you courage to improve, renew, or repair your own. Because it's never too late to develop better relationships with those we love.

HOW THE STORY BEGINS

OCTOBER THIRTEENTH. My sister Susie calls to break the news of my dad's sudden death. On impact, it feels as if my heart bursts open, spilling across my chest and exploding into my throat. I shriek out a few feeble cries then quiet myself to listen to the explanation, but I'm calm only on the outside. On the inside, I shake wildly. I am almost fifty years old, but it feels unimaginable. How could it be possible that he'd been struck by a car while crossing the road, killed instantly—right in front of my mom?

On that day, my whole world shifted. My Rock of Gibraltar fell into the sea. My father had embodied so many great qualities that I'd loved and learned from. In many ways he'd been a model for me, and I'd always been proud to call him my dad. He'd loved me unconditionally, and I'd always known it. That meant everything to me. It's what I clung to, what I kept remembering and reminding myself just after he died.

That isn't to say he was perfect, or that our family was flawless. Since his death I've found myself wishing I'd talked to him more about who he really was and what made him tick. My dad was an in-charge kind of man, and that usually made me feel stable and secure, but sometimes he went overboard—he had to be right, and we had to do it his way. I've since wondered, why did he get controlling like that? Did he ever think that might affect my confidence or ability to make decisions on my own? He treated me like a princess, but sometimes he treated my mom like she was incompetent. I still wonder why—it seemed groundless—yet she believed what he told her and went through her whole life feeling dumb. Since I can see myself in her, I've also struggled against believing I can't do the things I want to do in my life. I'm still perplexed by my father's bouts of depression, which he suffered when I was little, because my parents hid it and we never talked about it. Maybe our need to keep these dark feelings a secret is why we never talked much about most of our feelings when I was growing up, and why we could never share with anybody else what was really going on inside our family.

Even before that tragic October day, I'd already started a different way of parenting my two daughters. I didn't want them ever to wonder about their childhoods and my way of parenting. I didn't want them to start asking questions after I'd gone, because then it would be too late. I wanted to begin early on, while I could still answer their questions, explain my behaviors, listen to their complaints, and apologize for my screwups. Parent–child relationships are probably the most complicated ones on earth. I knew it was up to me to begin making ours as clean and forthright as possible.

I had no idea then how much it would pay off.

Dear Carol and Andrea,

As I think about how our story began, I remember that sunny afternoon one summer when we were up in the mountains at Lime Creek, having a picnic and playing along the water's edge. We were all so full of joy—happy to be in that most beautiful spot in nature and delighted to be together.

Andrea, I'm sure you were still in diapers. Carol, as a toddler, you suddenly looked up at me and said, "Mommy, I love you bushels and nightgowns!"

It was the most fanciful, spontaneous, and adorable exclamation to ever fly out of your tiny mouth, and one we have never let go of. I think now of how many cards, letters, and e-mails we have sent to each other over the years and signed with this little phrase you coined in the innocence of your childhood. After all these years, I still want you to know…

I love you bushels and nightgowns,

Mom

CHAPTER 1

Dooby-Dooby-Doo . . . Even Better than Sinatra Knew:

Developing a Relationship with Your Kids

ONE AFTERNOON MANY YEARS AGO, my first daughter, Carol, lay nursing in my arms, gazing into my face as if trying to determine who I was and what kind of mother I would be for her. I admit it was intimidating. I didn't know what to do when she cried; I couldn't figure out how to bathe her without letting her slip out of my hands into the water; I was afraid to trim her fingernails for fear of nipping her fingertips. I was thirty years old and glowing with love for her, but a rush of anxiety washed over me as I realized how little I knew about parenting a child. I felt alarm at the enormous responsibility of taking care of her and concern over whether I could provide her with what she'd need as she grew older. Like every new parent, I wanted to make her feel loved and secure. I thought about how I would discipline her—with flexibility and respect. I wanted to be like a life coach, guiding her through the maze of growing up, teaching her strong values and morals and helping to build her self-esteem so that she would be empowered to reach her potential. Most of all I wanted to build a close and trusting relationship with her so we could have mutual influence on each other and have tons of fun together throughout our lives.

Even as a novice mom, I was pretty sure I couldn't do it "right," that there was no such thing as a perfect parent or a flawless family. I could only try to do my best, as most parents do. But even though perfection would elude me, I thought I'd be able to go the extra mile for her, eagerly giving everything I had. I vowed I wouldn't use my position as her parent simply to exert power, take control, or boost my own ego. I believed I could be selfless enough to put myself in the background to help her reach her goals. I committed to talking with her, even though I feared I didn't have much wisdom or vast amounts of experience to deal with what would inevitably come up. I wouldn't be able to provide ready answers for difficult issues in life, such as a death in the family, a teenage pregnancy, problems with friends, or peers who started drinking, but I could always provide a safe forum in which to talk.

Yet even with my wholehearted commitment, the prospect of parenting was pretty frightening sometimes. I know I wasn't the only mom who was downright afraid that I'd fall short. I wasn't the only parent who felt like I didn't know how to do the biggest job I'd ever had. The title of one of Bruno Bettelheim's books, *A Good Enough Parent* (Vintage, 1988), has always encouraged me, because it implies that you don't have to be faultless. You can flail and even fail at times. As long as you have your sights on the goal of empowering your kids to be the best they can be, you can take solace in the notion that you're good enough.

And so it started a long time ago, when Carol and Andrea were just babies. I decided that *building a relationship with them* was the most important thing I could do as their parent. Somehow I knew it was the thing I wanted most.

Some parents don't understand the value of a relationship with their kids. Several years ago Bill and Sherry came into my office to discuss some marriage problems spurred by their sixteen-year-old daughter, Chloe. Bill was concerned that Chloe was beginning to strike out on her own, questioning the rules of the house and butting up against them from time to time. Sherry, on the other hand, felt Chloe was not out of line and that Bill was too strict. As a result of their differing parenting styles, they were in conflict with each other, and Chloe was stuck in the middle between a rigid dad and a waffling mom. She wanted to hide from her unreasonable father, but she received no positive message from her mother, so she was left to figure things out on her own.

Bill described how Chloe had friends over to hang out in their newly remodeled basement media room, but she didn't follow his rules about noise or curfew. His routine was to be uninvolved, then rush in at the last minute and mandate how things should be done. When Chloe went out, she wasn't always with the kids she said she'd be with and was occasionally fifteen to thirty minutes late returning home.

We talked about the concept of building a relationship with Chloe first as a basis for understanding better how to establish guidelines that fit for her. The idea resonated with Sherry immediately. She began to talk with Chloe in a nonjudgmental way, inviting Chloe to explain the circumstances surrounding each infraction of her dad's rules. Together they explored ways for Chloe to stay within the parameters they set together.

Bill, however, stuck tenaciously to his rules, reiterating that, as the dad, he was responsible for her well-being and had to have well-defined limits to protect her and ensure that she was being raised with the proper morals and values. He refused to open his mind to new thinking and wouldn't budge on his parenting role, and after a few sessions, he quit coming to therapy.

Sherry continued a while longer, even giving Chloe an opportunity to talk with me privately about her growing conflict with her dad. What a lovely young woman Chloe was. She had good common sense and an innate desire to do the right thing. After meeting with Chloe, I wanted to call Bill and tell him to get over it. He had a wonderful daughter, but he was so blinded by his rules that he couldn't even enjoy his good fortune.

> **EFFECTIVE PARENTING BEGINS WITH GOOD RELATIONSHIPS BETWEEN PARENTS AND THEIR CHILDREN.**

Much later, Chloe went off to college, then to law school, and then married a darling young man. The last I heard, she was living happily and successfully and maintaining the warmest and loveliest relationship with her mother. Bill missed out. He was disgruntled with his daughter while she lived at home, became even more distant from her after she left, and has only a cordial and stiff relationship with her now. What was the point?

Bill never understood that his most important parenting role was to build a loving and understanding relationship with his daughter. He flubbed the opportunity, while he had it, to share with his daughter his wisdom and experience, and so far, he hasn't figured out how to repair the damage. If Bill doesn't find a way to turn it around, maybe one day Chloe will be able to take the initiative to close the gap between them. No doubt there's a hole in her heart from missing her dad. Meanwhile, Bill still has a lot to learn—that effective parenting begins with good relationships between parents and their children.

Balance Doing and Being

One of my psychology professors, who encouraged us students to call him Charlie, taught me a lot by using unusual methods to get his point across. One day we were discussing the value of our own lives, and Charlie was advocating the balance between doing and being. Suddenly, as if he was channeling Frank Sinatra, he burst into the bridge of "Strangers in the Night." He crooned, "Dooby-dooby-doo . . ."

Charlie had a way of making something stick with you, and I've thought about his serenade often when considering the nature of parent–child relationships. Relationships are two-pronged—they require *doing* things with your kids and also just *being* with them. Charlie was onto something big. Dooby-dooby-doo . . . Even better than Sinatra knew!

Sometimes parents go overboard with activities, doing lots of things together, but that's only half of it. If you don't balance doing with the quiet times of just *being* together, you're missing the opportunity to get closer to your kids emotionally—to find out what they're thinking and what really makes them tick.

It's easy to hide behind sports and busy activities and never take the time to simply chat. Our kids have such a wide variety of needs that we should find ways to care for them and nurture them emotionally as well as physically. It's common for me to meet people in my practice who need to restore that balance, to take time to both do and be.

Even though you may be more comfortable with one than the other, there are two irreplaceable ways to build a relationship with your child—and you must do them both:

- Doing—caring for your child physically
- Being—caring for your child emotionally

These two components are the bedrock of parenting, the foundation you will build your relationship on. And your relationship will be the foundation of all your other efforts. So you can see how important it is to balance doing and being!

Relationship Builder #1: Doing

Doing is caring for your children physically, providing for and protecting them. It's the very first thing we need to do as parents, and most of us are drawn to it naturally.

Growing up, I enjoyed a close family with Mom, Dad, my older brother, and two younger sisters. My parents always prided themselves in how all of us stuck together. We defended and protected each other against anyone from the outside. We talked and laughed together, and we took family vacations together. We always ate long and happy family dinners together. Neighbor kids ran quickly home to eat and were back in our big backyard for the evening round of softball or kick the can almost before we had dug into our main course.

Mom was the most nurturing parent a child could ever hope for. She cared for us and tended to our every need. When we were kids, we'd sit regularly in the crook of her arm while she read stories to us— Peter Rabbit, Uncle Wiggily, Mother Goose. Our clothes were always perfectly ironed and hung in our closets. In high school we never left for a basketball game without a hot, home-cooked meal in our tummies. My dad was the most loving father a child could ever dream of. Every night after dinner I'd scramble onto his lap at the table while he read a chapter of the Bible to all of us. He often told me he would crawl through a sewer for me, and I always knew it was true. Yet, both of them felt more comfortable doing things for me than just being with me—

listening with open minds and nonjudgmental hearts, encouraging me to share whatever I had to say.

So, when I became a teenager, it seemed as if something was missing. I felt alone with no one to listen to me and understand my adolescent angst. As long as I was perfect, all went well, but the moment I had an imperfect thought, I believed I had no one to share it with. I wondered about so many things: growing up, boys, sex, life. Despite all the talk about being a close-knit family, I didn't feel comfortable sharing any of my "stuff" with my parents. I didn't want them to know I had any feelings or concerns, and I was ashamed about the natural changes occurring in my physical and emotional being during those years.

We definitely had a positive relationship, but it wasn't enough help to me when my own difficulties, questions, and confusions came bubbling up. I wish I'd had a *deeper* relationship with them. I needed someone who really understood me.

Relationship Builder #2: Being

Being is more elusive than doing—it's about caring for your children emotionally, not just physically. I first thought about the concept of being before I was a therapist, before I even had much experience as a parent. I began to think about Carol and Andrea going through something similar to my adolescent turmoil when they were still small. I wondered how it would work if we three started early trying to create that profound relationship I'd wanted, before the two of them could even totally grasp what we were doing. Then, when they were older, the relationship would be firmly in place, rooted so deeply that nothing could undermine it, chip away at it, or destroy it. When their own trials and troubles appeared, I hoped we'd already be so accustomed to talking openly about everything that it would seem only natural for them to talk to me about the difficult stuff.

I didn't know any rules for being a parent but I decided to try building a strong connection with each of my kids and to make that my primary parenting goal. In fact, this was the only trick in my bag. This would be the foundation of every interaction between us. It ended up guiding my decisions on how to talk with them and how to discipline them. Every mom and dad knows that parenting can be confusing and frustrating. It's a downright wild ride! Situations come up, and you have absolutely no idea how to handle them. And somehow, no two kids are ever alike, so you can't always learn anything useful from the older child's experience that will apply to the younger. Every drama seems to be a new trauma.

Having some kind of basis from which to handle parenting seemed comforting to me. Gradually, as my kids grew older and I learned more, the relationship became the filter through which I evaluated and employed all other parenting styles or theories. If a particular intervention didn't build the relationship overall, I'd think twice before implementing it.

One evening when Carol and Andrea were six and four years old, I decided that I should explain my burgeoning idea of relationship-focused parenting to them, even though I hadn't really fleshed it out yet. Standing in the kitchen in front of our huge stove with the six burners and the griddle big enough to make twenty pancakes at once, I began like this, as they turned their small faces up to me in typical inquisitive fashion: "You don't know it yet, but one day you'll realize that I have very little power over you. Right now it seems like I'm in charge—that my job is to tell you what to do and not to do and that your job is to obey—but that's only true as long as you *believe* it's true."

They looked at me with question marks on their faces. *Huh? What is she talking about?* Of course I was talking over their heads, but I figured that at least my idea was out on the table. We could always come back to it when they could understand more.

I pressed on and confessed that my power over them was really an illusion. If they decided not to obey me, I'd be in a tough spot. Oh yes, I could discipline them by giving them a time-out, not allowing them to have dessert, restricting their favorite activity, even spanking them, but that wouldn't necessarily guarantee obedience. More important, the older they got, the less effective my power would become, as they developed the ability to do what they wanted to do without me.

I suggested my still-rudimentary concept of how to structure our family. I told them that I loved the idea of building our family around the core principle of the relationship, to always maintain intimate contact. I wanted to

> I LOVED THE IDEA OF BUILDING OUR FAMILY AROUND THE CORE PRINCIPLE OF THE RELATIONSHIP, TO ALWAYS MAINTAIN INTIMATE CONTACT.

start building this relationship right away so that it would be the bedrock of our entire lives together. I would do my best to parent them with respect, sensitivity, and courtesy. I hoped they would respond to me in kind because they trusted me, my belief in them, and my love for them.

They remained quizzical the whole time I talked to them. That was okay. I thought it was better to say it too early than too late. It's highly unlikely either of them even remembers that conversation, but for me it was a landmark in settling the definition and parameters of our parent–child relations. It also solidified in my mind that I would always try to talk with my daughters, that no topic would be off-limits, and that I would do my best to support them emotionally.

The balance between doing and being is hard to maintain, and I think I was better at the being part than the doing part. But just as doing is necessary for a child's physical welfare, so is being for her long-term emotional health.

From Theory to Practice

I developed and used this parenting theory in my work as a psychotherapist. In my practice, struggling parents often came to see me for advice on how to deal with kids going through difficult times. Rather than giving them a menu of principles—one for this problem, one for that—I'd say the following: "We're going to approach this from the perspective of how you might build a relationship with your child that creates a strong connection and close contact. My theory is that when both you and your child believe in the power of the relationship, almost all situations can be resolved through open and honest talking. We'll confront issues and work through problems, create limits and explore consequences, find effective discipline strategies and strengthen communication skills, and we'll stay directed by our constant belief in a strong and healthy relationship between you and your child."

As the years rolled on and Carol and Andrea grew from childhood into adolescence into adulthood, I continued to put my theory into practice in our family and I shared with them the details of how I parented them. I want them to know what I did and why so they can be more aware when their time comes to parent their own children. Not that I always knew what I was doing. Sometimes I flew by the seat of my pants, but I was always guided by the underlying principle of nurturing my relationship with them.

In hindsight, I realize my original concept was crude—a smattering of an idea, a rough sketch—because, not yet having raised them, I had no concept of what lay ahead. Over time my underlying notion of relationship took a firmer shape. Today I understand that it was more complex than I thought at the beginning. Nuances and intricacies arose as my girls grew up and continued to present new and challenging issues.

Initially, there was only one reason I wanted to create an intimate relationship with the two of them: I imagined it would result in a position of friendship and trust between us where I could guide and counsel them through their problems and have fun with them at the same time. Back then I didn't even know there was a second reason. I knew very little about the power of my influence in their lives, and certainly not the extent to which our relationship would help mold and sculpt their very destinies. As it turns out, that was the more important reason. It's why I hope you'll take this book to heart and seize the incredible opportunity you have right now to make the biggest difference in your child's life.

You know parenting offers no guarantees. You can't control your children's destinies, and you don't have ultimate control over their choices, but you do have an opportunity to walk side by side, talk with one another, offer your guidance through difficult times, and be a mentor and a coach. What you say and how you interact with children impacts how they think about and believe in themselves. How you treat them knocks them down or builds them up. As a parent or stepparent, no doubt you feel the enormous responsibility—the moral obligation—to teach your children about life and the world around them. A good relationship is the bridge that will keep you connected to your kids and earn you the privilege of helping them excel in their endeavors.

If you don't have relationship building in the forefront of your mind, you can easily get sidetracked in a moment of crisis. A dear friend recently reminded me of a conversation we had many years ago. He'd separated from his wife and was experiencing the wrath of his adolescent son, who was rude and insolent with him, blaming him for ripping the family apart. He was so upset by his son's angry accusations that he wanted to yell back at him. He was tempted to tell the boy the pathetic truth about his mom, explaining some of the sad details of their dysfunctional marriage. He wanted to kick the boy out of the house and send him to live with his mom just to get away from his nasty behavior. My friend reminded me that I had given him some good advice back then.

I told him, no—do *not* act on any of your emotions or you will surely regret it. Your son is going through a really tough time; you both are, but now you need to protect and nurture your relationship so it can span this confusing, grieving period of your lives and so that the boy will continue to talk with you. You should set boundaries, I encouraged. Tell your son what is acceptable behavior and what is not, and try to understand his anger. If things get really hot, you should tell your son you're going to leave the room and come back later when you and he are both calmer. Don't push him away now or he'll go talk to somebody else. He has a right to his anger—his family has been torn apart. Just don't say or do anything that would harm your relationship.

My friend said he heeded my advice and is so glad he did. He was grateful to be able to hold onto the principle of relationship building so he could keep his interactions with his son on track and not get diverted by his own rash emotions. It got them both through that really tough period, and they developed a wonderfully intimate and caring relationship, instead of letting pain and chaos overcome them.

Stay Awake at the Wheel

It's never too late to develop a relationship with your child. But it's far easier if you haven't neglected the relationship beforehand or led it off in the wrong direction. Of course, for most parents, it's hard to tell where we take the turn to the wrong road. My dear friend and mentor Mae Page once told me that our failings as parents usually occur in areas outside our awareness. Most parents are trying to do their best, so when we notice that any of our actions and behaviors are not uplifting for our kids, we try to change what we're doing. That means it's the things about which we have no conscious awareness that get us into trouble in our parenting. Let's say I'm still angry at my dad for mistreating me when I was a kid, or maybe I'm uptight in my sexual attitudes because my ex-husband was unfaithful to me, or maybe I learned low self-esteem from spending my childhood with a mom who thought she was dumb and incompetent. These attitudes and feelings seep out invisibly into my own home and soak into my children as they grow up—all without me knowing it. We pass on, from generation to generation, the legacies of our parents and grandparents and the baggage from other relationships in our lives.

Perhaps Bill, Chloe's dad, was simply trying to raise his daughter as he had learned from his own parents. Maybe he was just stumbling through life trying to manage his own struggles, pains, and problems, and his daughter ambled into the line of fire. You can see how important it is to know yourself well and be working out your own problems as you start building relationships with your kids.

A couple of years ago, another dad came to see me for help in dealing with his teenage daughter. George had been divorced from Erin's mom for many years, and Erin had lived with her mom. As a single parent, George buried himself in his work, visiting his daughter on occasional weekends and holidays. Mom got very busy rebuilding her social life and had hardly any time to devote to a child. Erin hung on pretty well for several years until she came upon the snares of adolescence. She started disobeying her mom, dating boys several years older, sneaking out of the house at night, and using drugs in her own bedroom with friends. Mom finally noticed what was happening and tried to take control, but was slammed with defiance and dishonesty. In despair, Mom threw up her hands, called George, and said, "She's yours."

After years of hardly any contact, George suddenly inherited a rebellious teenager with a surly attitude, bad language, and fuchsia hair. What could he do?

He could have set stringent rules and demanded compliance, but when his daughter disobeyed him, what would he do next? I suggested that much of Erin's over-the-top behavior might be a call for help: *Please notice me. Please pay attention to me. Please come alongside me.* Her behavior might also be a test to see if her parents would abandon her altogether if she behaved badly enough. Poor Erin had never really had a relationship she could count on with either her mom or her dad. Most of all, she needed a relationship with her dad that she could trust, one that wouldn't go away if she misbehaved or got into trouble. Among other things, I told George he needed to learn how to be there for his daughter—over the long haul.

Starting so late in the game, George had a long row to hoe. He was like the guy who had fallen asleep at the wheel and driven off the road, over the shoulder, down into the ditch and up the other side, through the fence, across the field, and into the trees, coming to a stop only when he splashed into the stream. He knew exactly where he belonged but it was a long, bumpy way back. First he had to get out of the stream and turn around. Then he had to pick his way through the trees, bump back across the field, scratch through the fence, clunk down into the ditch and up the other side, roll back over the shoulder, then drive up onto the road.

George is tenacious. He's trying and he's not giving up. After many years of not being involved with his daughter, he decided to create a strong connection with her. It's never too late to start building a relationship with your kids, but the more troubled they are when you begin, the more difficult the journey. Last I heard, George had come out of the trees and was rumbling along back across the field. I wish him luck.

> IN PARENTING YOU DON'T HAVE TO KNOW HOW TO DO IT RIGHT. YOU JUST HAVE TO KNOW WHEN YOU'VE FALLEN ASLEEP AT THE WHEEL. YOU HAVE TO BE ABLE TO FEEL THE DIFFERENCE BETWEEN BEING IN BALANCE AND OFF BALANCE WITH YOUR KIDS.

In parenting you don't have to know how to do it right. You just have to know when you've fallen asleep at the wheel. You have to be able to feel the difference between being in balance and off balance with your kids. When you get off balance on a ski slope, you put your arms forward and shift your weight to the balls of your feet. When you get off balance riding western saddle horseback, you put your feet in front of you and lean back. When you get off balance with your kids, you fall back onto the relationship.

Everything else builds from the relationship. You don't have to have the answers. You may not even understand the questions. There's no right way to do it. You just create an environment in which there is freedom to talk, discuss opinions, and express feelings.

Shifts Happen

As much attention as I put on the relationship, sometimes I talk to parents who are afraid that a good relationship with their children will be destroyed if anything changes. Life is full of changes. Natural or unexpected, catastrophic or happy—each one can throw off the balance in your family, leaving your kids uncertain, confused, or even frightened. That's when you need to tighten your connection with them, stay engaged, talk about the changes, and be available to support them. Talk with them openly and let them know that changes are an inevitable part of life. Don't minimize their feelings or make them feel immature or foolish for being unsure at an uncertain time. Most of all, assure them that you'll be there beside them and that, together, you can all make it through to the other side and come out even stronger.

LIFE IS FULL OF CHANGES. NATURAL OR UNEXPECTED, CATASTROPHIC OR HAPPY—EACH ONE CAN THROW OFF THE BALANCE IN YOUR FAMILY, LEAVING YOUR KIDS UNCERTAIN, CONFUSED, OR EVEN FRIGHTENED.

I still remember the first time I dropped Carol off at the end of our road to be gobbled up by the big yellow monster that would drive her to kindergarten. Her little legs stretched to reach each step, and I gulped as she disappeared inside the school bus. When the door closed and the bus drove away, I watched until it turned the corner, and then I burst into tears. It was a shift for all of us. A new era had begun. Carol would spend most of her days away from me, and she would begin to be influenced more by teachers and peers. I sensed that I would have to make sure to set aside special times to be with her so that the relationship we'd built when she was a toddler would continue to flourish. This was when peer pressure would begin to take root.

We were lucky to live in the Rocky Mountains where we could take advantage of the beautiful outdoors together year round. We hiked and fished, camped and skied—all activities that allowed us time to be together having fun and growing closer. This part of family life was easy for us, and at times it felt idyllic.

I also remember the pain, chaos, and confusion of living with my then-husband, who was an addict. It was tumultuous and, at times, terrifying. When Carol and Andrea were very young I was too horrified and humiliated to talk about it with anyone at all. Following the patterns established in my childhood—especially the policy that families keep their own counsel—I tried to deny that there was a problem. In hindsight, I'm so sorry for that. I know my daughters suffered more from the secrets and the silence than they did from the circumstances.

When my ex-husband's addiction finally came out into the open, he began to seek treatment, and my kids and I started to talk about it at last. For the first time in my life, I was learning to reveal my own and my family's vulnerabilities. It was particularly difficult because I had grown up believing you should never divulge family weaknesses or failings, and I discovered that it's really hard to change and heal if you can't talk about your problems with anyone.

When Carol and Andrea were just six and four, we began to engage in many, many conversations about drugs and alcohol. It felt good. Releasing our family secrets was beneficial for all of us. I learned many years ago that it isn't what happens to you that harms you as much as *not dealing* with what happens to you. I know that all our talking over the course of many years helped them to heal from the damage of spending their early childhood in a family with one addict, their daddy, and one enabler, me.

Then came the divorce, an event that threw us all upside down again. That was when, as a single mom, I began my psychotherapy career, joining the ranks of working parents who were consumed with juggling home life and work life. Like millions of moms, I tried to figure out how to cram it all in and still have time with my daughters. I had no idea how I could do it all, but somehow I remembered my commitment to myself to prioritize my bond with Carol and Andrea, so I tried to think up fun outings where we could spend our days and nights together.

One of our first excursions as a threesome was a camping trip with several families in the desert in Utah, something that had become an annual event over Mother's Day. It felt very different that time, though, because their father and I had always set up camp while the girls took off to play in the desert. During this trip my daughters and I became a team. Without even being asked, Carol and Andrea helped me every inch of the way, putting up the tent, getting out the cooking gear, and organizing our campsite. I was so proud of them for being responsible and mature enough to see the need and pitch in. It confirmed for me that we were a family and we would stick together. We'd be okay.

On Mother's Day morning they awakened me, excited to give me their gift. They took my hand and led me across gullies and behind sand hills, pointing as we walked along to each individual desert flower they'd selected the day before. Since each flower was so delicate and beautiful, they hadn't wanted to pick any of them. I gathered them together in my mind's eye and envisioned the most beautiful bouquet. It was my best Mother's Day present ever. That weekend I knew for sure that we would make it through thick and thin. We were a family. We were the three of us.

The first time I put them on a plane as unaccompanied minors to go visit their dad, I thought I might crumble from the loneliness of being without them for two whole months. This was a huge shift for all of us. Peering through the airport window, I watched as they walked onto the tarmac and up the stairs of the prop jet. I waved and waved, hoping they could see me through the darkened window at their seats. Then I ran outside to watch the plane roll down the runway and take off. I squinted into the sunny blue sky until their plane became only a speck in the distance. My throat tightened and tears welled up in my eyes. I stood for a moment longer, prayed for their safety, and then felt the sudden shift inside me. I had my own life to live as they had theirs. We each needed to get on with it and enjoy the moments we had before us. Actually, I felt my whole body relax, relieved of the constant responsibility of being a single parent. We would all have a good summer, we would connect every day by phone, and when it was over we would have even more to share with each other.

During the five years I was single, we went through a lot together. From my research to develop the parenting courses I taught at our local community college when they were in middle school, I learned much that augmented my own parenting experiences with them. However, no academic study could really prepare me for their inevitable transfer to high school and all the adjustments of arriving at a new school right at the onset of adolescence. It seemed as if everything was unfamiliar and unsettling. As Carol, and then Andrea, wandered through the maze of high school, our trusting and unfailing relationship kept us exploring, analyzing, and reviewing the issues. I tried to notice their daily moods and be available to them when I saw something in their demeanor or tone of voice that alerted me to any negative feelings in them. Instead of ignoring those feelings and behaviors or assuming they were normal signs of adolescence, I decided to talk with them. Not by interrogating them, but by being gentle and caring. It was the time for me to learn to be open, to listen more than I talked, and certainly not to spurt out judgments or strong opinions that might close them down. From parties, classes, boyfriends, sports, teachers, and school activities to beliefs, questions, curiosities, and feelings—we discussed it all. I hoped I would continue to be the person they felt comfortable talking with.

FROM PARTIES, CLASSES, BOYFRIENDS, SPORTS, TEACHERS, AND SCHOOL ACTIVITIES TO BELIEFS, QUESTIONS, CURIOSITIES, AND FEELINGS—WE DISCUSSED IT ALL.

Then came another shift: I met and fell in love with Terry. Carol was sixteen and Andrea was fourteen. At the time I didn't even understand the potential problems of a stepdad entering the picture. Terry must have, though, because he worked hard to develop his own relationship with them. He never pushed his way into our family; he was sensitive about the existing relationship between my daughters and me, and he was careful not to assume a position of priority or control.

I'm still working on my relationships with my stepsons. Because they were older than Carol and Andrea and already off to college when I met their dad, it was much more difficult than I would have thought to get close to them. I know blended families aren't easy, but I had fantasized that ours would grow into one united family, like the Brady Bunch. Now I realize that it's more difficult (though definitely not impossible) to develop something tightly knit if you're not able to start when your kids are young. I learned that there's huge value in starting early and never giving up. Over time, my relationships with Terry's sons keep getting better, and they know that I'm committed to them.

Relationships require constant attention, and sustaining them requires time and effort. The path of least resistance is to allow a relationship to dissolve and slip away, especially when you're scrambling to keep up with changes in the family. No matter how big or little the shifts, the important thing is to continue to grow and nurture the bonds you've built with your kids so they do not falter or fail—even in times of change.

One of Those Days

At times, though, the biggest obstacle to your relationship with your children isn't the constant changes of life, the difficulty of seeing yourself clearly, or anything else controllable—it's the days where you just lose perspective and mess up. In case you're thinking that I pretend to have been the perfect mom, I'll tell you one of my low moments in motherhood—an example of a parenting mistake Carol remembers, too, as an awful experience. We've talked about it many times since then, and I've apologized to her over and over. Thank goodness, she has forgiven me.

It might surprise you that this "bad parenting day" happened over something relatively trivial. My daughter didn't break the law or do anything immoral. But even the most diligent parents, with the best intentions, can forget their way and make mistakes over the stupidest things. This story should show you that these errors in judgment and behavior can be corrected and the relationship can be preserved if you show some humility and respect for your child.

It was the summer between Carol's junior and senior years at Northwestern University, and she'd taken an internship in San Francisco, city of phenomenal fog, fabulous food, frivolous fun, and alternative ideas. One evening several days before I was to visit, she called me to announce that she'd decided to pierce her nose before I arrived. Of course, she knew I had a *thing* about unusually placed piercings (not so much on other people, but definitely on my daughters).

I know, I know—in the grand scheme of things, having a daughter who pierces her nose doesn't exactly constitute a family crisis, but at the time I went into instant "I've been stabbed" mode, exploded in anger, and then I pleaded. Carol was quite calm but resolute. She wasn't calling to ask my permission. She was an adult and going to do what she was going to do.

With both my daughters, once they were adults, our conversations were usually more a matter of sharing what we were thinking about and planning to do. If one of us didn't agree, it was cause to stop and rethink because we always valued each other's input. We also valued the mutual support and validation an agreement provided, like a kind of strong backbone holding us up before we made a leap into the unknown. Yet this particular evening, Carol and I had a very unsatisfactory, going-nowhere conversation and decided to talk again the following day.

I went to bed and tossed and turned, flipped and flopped, groaned and heaved. *How could she,* I moaned to myself, *when she knows how much I hate that?* Since I couldn't sleep anyway, I decided to get up and write in my journal, a technique I often recommend to my therapy clients to get their feelings out.

The idea is to write without lifting your pen, so you can write without editing anything. Just letting the words flow, tumbling from the gut, allowing the raw feelings to spill without thinking about how they're coming out or what they sound like—out from the bowels of your belly, where they're overpowering your ability to sleep, relax, think, talk, or behave reasonably—can do wonders for a troubled mind. I call it verbal vomit. Get those words out. They're toxic on the inside and totally benign on the outside—as long as you splat them down on paper and not onto another person. The idea is to detoxify yourself, not harm someone else with your poisonous words. So you write, then you burn or tear up the paper, or tuck it away in a safe place where no one else will ever read it. Once the ripping, roaring, raw emotions are out and you've given yourself a little time to calm down, you're cleaned out a bit and free to think rationally. Now you can choose carefully how you want to discuss the real issues that are still left and important to resolve.

> GET THOSE WORDS OUT. THEY'RE TOXIC ON THE INSIDE AND TOTALLY BENIGN ON THE OUTSIDE— AS LONG AS YOU SPLAT THEM DOWN ON PAPER AND NOT ONTO ANOTHER PERSON.

That's where I made my mistake. As soon as I finished writing, I called Carol. Unfortunately for both of us, she answered the phone. Still in the heat of my toxic emotions, I read to her—yes, *read* to her—what I'd written. Oh, God in heaven, what a horrible thing to do to anyone, especially to my daughter, whom I love with all my heart.

Carol must have frozen in shock and horror. She has the most gentle and loving heart, and I still get tears in my eyes thinking about how my words must have hurt her. I've prayed that both she and I would forget what I said, but I still remember that most of the letter was about how I believed she was trying to hurt me. How self-centered I was to think her behaviors had anything to do with me!

(In my defense—a tiny little bit of defense—kids certainly do all kinds of things just to get back at their parents. Sometimes they do them intentionally, but often their behavior is subconscious. A perfect way to take a stab at a parent is to rebel. If kids want to register a disagreement with what a parent wants for them, they can do something blatantly different. If they'd like to show displeasure with who that parent is, then they can do something obvious that the parent would never do. But that is a digression.)

After I finished reading the letter, Carol began to cry. She said she'd like to hang up then because she couldn't think of anything to say that would not be hurtful to me. She added that she would call me in the morning, after she'd had time to think.

Bless her for being 100 percent more mature than her mother was at that moment.

I mumbled some feeble good-byes and hung up, finally realizing I'd just done a terrible thing. I sat there in my office, weeping, thoughts racing in every direction, grieving over how I'd wounded Carol and frantically trying to think of what to do next.

I knew my emotions weren't really justified, but feelings aren't necessarily logical. People feel what they feel. Understanding and accepting your own irrational feelings is the first step toward being able to handle your children's feelings without blaming, judging, or trying to talk them out of having them. Of course, responsibly dealing with your own emotions never includes dumping them on someone else, and I'd just done exactly that.

If I couldn't sleep before, I couldn't even lie down now. Was there any way to repair this? Would Carol ever even speak to me again, let alone be a daughter to me? Believe me, words *do* matter. Once you've said them, you can't pull them back in. You can apologize and try to go on, but the cuts from the words are still there.

I was sitting awake, head in hands, some thirty minutes later when the phone rang: "Mom, I can't go to sleep with this thing between us. We've always been able to talk about everything, and I'm just too sad to let it go until morning."

Oh, thank you, God. Carol cares about us, and she's given me another chance. When I wasn't able to focus on the relationship, my daughter was. She'd taken the principle I'd tried to maintain throughout her childhood so well to heart that she was able to use it to deal with me when I did something wrong.

Well, one good thing about me: I'm a master apologizer. I was completely humbled that my daughter had better skills than I did to work through this difficult situation. We talked. Carol assured me that this was not a rebellious act against me—it was just a cool thing to do for a while, and when she was over it, she'd take the nose ring out. I assured her that I loved her more than I could ever find the words to express and that if there were any way to eradicate the past two hours from our lives, I'd do it in an instant. I found a thousand ways to say "I'm sorry." While I still didn't like the idea of anything marring her sweet little nose, I'd find a way to manage. We finally hung up our phones, hugging each other across the miles, and I fell into bed thoroughly exhausted. Carol must have done the same.

I arrived in San Francisco a few days later and spied the tiniest diamond stud discreetly peeking out from the side of Carol's nose. If I had not disliked it so much, I would have had to admit it was kind of cute.

In truth, I was actually proud of her tenacity with me. I'm sure I, like any parent, can seem ominously powerful at times, and I'd never want my child to be so intimidated that she couldn't stand up to me or think for herself. In the end, it was probably good for both of us to establish that Carol would be living her own life, thank you, and not kowtowing to me or anyone else. I admired her—although I confess that when her nose got infected a couple months later, I was secretly glad, hoping it would be the impetus to remove the stud. She wore that darned thing all the way through graduation and removed it only when she was job hunting and thought it might make the wrong statement about who she was to a prospective employer.

> **AS PARENTS WE *DO* MAKE MISTAKES, SO IT'S IMPORTANT TO LEARN HOW TO GET THROUGH THE BAD TIMES. AND IF YOUR KIDS HAVE THE EXPERIENCE OF A STRONG RELATIONSHIP WITH YOU, THEY CAN EVEN HELP IN THE RECOVERY.**

What's the moral of my story? You can avoid my horrible feelings of guilt if you're respectful to your kids at all times, sensitive to their feelings, and try not to ever hurt them. But be quick to apologize if (and when!) you mess up.

As parents we *do* make mistakes, so it's important to learn how to get through the bad times. And if your kids have the experience of a strong relationship with you, they can even help in the recovery.

Recently, a mom came to my therapy office to talk about her son Ryan. She and her husband (Ryan's stepdad) had always believed in having a strong relationship with their kids, and they had all enjoyed open communication and a lot of fun times together. Now, at seventeen, Ryan had suddenly clammed up and become uncooperative. He responded to his mom with uncaring comments and was unwilling to participate in family activities. She was disappointed, hurt, and angry, and she vacillated between wanting to turn her back on him and wanting to really give him a piece of her mind. As we talked, I reminded her that this is when those seventeen years of relationship become really valuable. Instead of telling him off and attacking him for being so disrespectful to the family, I urged her to talk with him about their relationship—how important it is to her, what has happened to it, and how that makes her feel. She should explain her feelings not in a way that would make him feel guilty but in a way that would let him know how much she loves him and misses him when he's not a part of the family. Remember, when you get off balance with your kids, you fall back onto the relationship.

The result? She did. And Ryan began to talk about how he was struggling in his relationship with his real dad and having problems with his friends. Not knowing how to handle either situation, he lost faith that anyone cared about him and just shut off from everyone. Ryan and his mom quickly got back on track.

Don't be afraid to talk with your kids when you sense things aren't right. But instead of assuming and criticizing, share how you feel and what you'd like to do to correct the problem between you. Most of all, be sure to create a rock-solid relationship with your kids, because when the tempests roll, the winds rage, and the waves crash over the surface, the relationship has to be strong enough that its very essence remains undamaged by the storms.

Dear Carol and Andrea,

I know a lot of kids don't talk to their parents—especially when they're teenagers—but we always did.

I confess there were times when I almost wished you HADN'T shared with me, like when you'd done something wrong or when I felt like you gave me TOO MUCH information.

Then I had to figure out how to deal with what you'd told me, and often I didn't know how. Honestly, sometimes ignorance is bliss!

But, overall, believe me, we are blessed to have the relationships we've always had. I know being open with each other has been such a benefit for all of us.

I love you bushels and nightgowns,

Mom

CHAPTER 2

When in Doubt, Talk It Out:

Learning How to Communicate

I T'S IMPORTANT TO TALK WITH YOUR KIDS at every phase of their development and at every stage of their burgeoning independence. I hope you never lose your ability to communicate with your kids—even when you feel inadequate—because communication is at the top of the list of essential parenting tools. I tried to start when my daughters were still babies with the goal of never stopping.

In contrast, I remember a client of mine, Jessica, with both fondness and sadness. Her parents didn't understand the value of having a relationship with her and didn't have a clue about how to communicate with her. She was twelve years old when she came to see me, a troubled girl who looked and acted a lot older than she was. She routinely snuck out of her house and hitchhiked the twenty miles or so into town because she usually had no money for the bus. Then she met up with her friends, who were easily five to ten years older than she was, and haunted the local hangout spots. Clustered in tight little groups, they smoked cigarettes, passed joints, and slugged booze from well-hidden bottles.

As the night wore on, Jessica would slip away into some guy's pick-up truck, go to his apartment, and have sex. Different guys on different nights. Sex with anybody who'd have her. On the outside Jessica looked tough, but on the inside she was lonely, starving for a relationship, and needing connection, so she connected in the only way she knew—with her body.

Because she was precocious, Jessica had few friends at school. Because she lived on a different planet from her parents, she had zero family life at home. She desperately needed someone to talk to and feel comfortable with. She craved a place to relax, be herself, and fit in. Since she had no hope of finding any of these things with her family, she went to town and, like a chameleon, changed herself to match the scene, blend into the environment, and find a niche where she could feel like she belonged.

Meanwhile, back home, Jessica's parents occasionally discovered that she was missing, but they had no idea how to handle the situation except to ground her soundly when she finally returned, locking her in her bedroom with no TV, no phone, and no music. Of course, Jessica had long since discovered the window, so she simply snuck out again and hightailed it back to town, where she tried to bury her pain in the attention of her friends. By the time her parents brought her to see me, the patterns were well established.

This story is only partially about Jessica. She was merely the child in a dysfunctional, noncommunicative family, playing out her part as perfectly as if it had been scripted. The story should really focus on her parents, because they're the ones who held most of the power. They hadn't communicated with their daughter, listened to her, shown interest in her feelings or needs, or made her feel special or cherished. They were fine, upstanding people who had high moral standards, strict Christian values, and a clear vision of how Jessica should behave. That was actually part of the problem. They knew not only how she should behave but also how she should think, what she should believe, how she should look, and who she should be. They didn't know much about feelings, so they weren't very concerned about how she might feel, other than to think she should feel content to follow their rules and obey their directives.

Jessica's parents seemed to be clueless about how to connect with their daughter. Somewhere inside them they felt love for her, but they didn't understand her as a young woman and had no skills for talking with her or listening to her. They only knew how to talk *at* her, lay down the law, impose punishments, get angry, and then get silent at her disobedience. Whenever Jessica tried to describe her desires, express her feelings, or explain her own reasoning, her parents froze. It was as if they were stunned and horrified that their child had thoughts or needs of her own. Like statues, Jessica's parents gave her empty stares with no responses and no solutions. They were stuck with their rebellious adolescent and had no tools to begin to work through their problems.

Jessica's parents didn't understand that their lack of communication was closely linked to her low self-esteem, and that to build it up she had to find people who *would* talk with her, enjoy her, and accept her. The parents' terse, uptight interaction with their daughter was actually driving her to the very behaviors and friends they loathed— word by word.

Every time they told her what to do and what not to do without listening to what she wanted or why, they gave her a message that she didn't matter, chipping out yet another chunk of her self-worth. Every time they made decisions for her without consulting her, they made her feel small and insignificant, tearing away another piece of her self-image. Every time they punished her without asking for her side of the story, they disparaged and depreciated her, depriving her of more of her self-respect. What they had taken away from her with their poor communication, they could have repaired with good communication, but they didn't.

Instead, they sent her to see me.

I liked Jessica a lot, and we became close. If ever there was a girl who desperately needed connection, conversation, and acceptance, she was the one. I found her quite easy to talk with, but of course, I was doing a lot of listening and no judging. She was very bright and interesting, especially for a young woman of her age, and I was fascinated by her thoughts, opinions, and slant on the world. We talked about all kinds of things—whatever came up was fodder for conversation. We explored her ideas together, we discussed benefits and consequences of her behaviors, and we gently dove into the realm of her feelings.

Jessica rarely missed a session. I think she looked forward to the refuge of my office. The more she came to trust that I wouldn't hurt or punish her, the more she opened up the dark caves of her inner life to me. Over time she began to ask me for my opinions; she wanted my advice. I felt I was beginning to give her a new perspective on herself and on relationships with adults, as well as a new vision of what life could be like for her in the world outside my office. The changes were happening simply because we were communicating. Because of our communication, we were building a relationship that made a huge difference in Jessica's life.

Old forces still loomed large when she went home; nothing was changing for Jessica there. She still craved the nonjudgmental acceptance of her parents. She still needed to be seen by them as the person she was, rather than the person they wanted her to be. She still longed for them to talk *with* her instead of *at* her, but her parents never thought they needed help for themselves, so they never learned how to change and grow to meet the needs of their daughter. They stayed pressed inside their rigid world, peering out myopically at the frightening scene Jessica was forcing upon them. I believe their own fears prevented them from expanding their inflexible, unyielding views of child rearing.

When they finally came to my office to talk about Jessica, I pleaded with them to loosen up and bolster her self-esteem by honoring her with interested conversation. I asked them to come toward their daughter in love and acceptance rather than continually maintaining the wall of rules between them. No, I didn't ask them to condone Jessica's behavior. Her behavior was inappropriate at best and downright wrong and even illegal at worst. I didn't ask them to remove the rules or the consequences for disobedience. She needed structure and boundaries. I asked them to soften, to try to get inside *her* feelings, to listen to *her*, to express caring and concern, to help her feel good about herself—in a word, to communicate. But they continued to sit on the sofa in my office, frozen. They were anxious yet unyielding, unwilling to entertain the idea of creating a home environment of open dialogue and nonthreatening conversation.

> **I ASKED THEM TO COME TOWARD THEIR DAUGHTER IN LOVE AND ACCEPTANCE RATHER THAN CONTINUALLY MAINTAINING THE WALL OF RULES BETWEEN THEM.**

Although we were making good headway with Jessica's therapy, her world outside my office kept pulling her back. More than once I was asked to help negotiate between her and her juvenile officer. Once her parents called me in wild desperation and, right or wrong, I sped to her house to try to avert a runaway.

One afternoon she walked into my office, and she had shorn half her hair. Right down the middle from front to back—left side long, right side shaved. My only comment was, "Do you think that will get you the attention you want?" She was not a bad girl. She was a girl in deep trouble, trying as best she knew how to get her needs for love, support, and acceptance met. No matter what she did, her parents never learned how to step up to the plate.

In the end, Jessica went to live in a foster home until she graduated from high school. There was palpable love, a relaxed atmosphere, and plenty of communication with her foster parents, but I don't think she was there long enough to overcome the first fourteen years of her life in a strict, stifled family. She started college and had to work simultaneously to pay her bills, but she dropped out to get married because she was pregnant.

Although I've lost track of Jessica, I think of her from time to time because her story makes me sad. Obviously, I cannot compare being her therapist to being her parent, but I know what inroads I was able to make by communicating with her with acceptance, respect, and understanding. There is no doubt in my mind that if her parents had been able to do the same, Jessica's life would not have taken such difficult twists and turns.

Most kids won't talk to their parents if their parents don't talk to them. Why would they? Communication is a two-way street—a give and take—and it's the bedrock of a relationship. It's what holds families together. Jessica's parents lost their child because they never understood this most basic principle of parenting.

Get to the Heart of Communication

Many books have been written about communication skills, and I don't want to duplicate what can be read elsewhere. I do want to share what worked for my daughters and me, and what's worked for many of my therapy clients. And that is one simple rule: *When in doubt, talk it out.* It means so much to be able to talk openly and freely about anything at all—and it can turn out to be the most valuable thing you do together. I know it was that way in our family.

WHEN IN DOUBT, TALK IT OUT. IT MEANS SO MUCH TO BE ABLE TO TALK OPENLY AND FREELY ABOUT ANYTHING AT ALL.

You can see talking as a way to get to know your children better, to support them more fully, to help them explore and solve their problems, and to have more fun with them. Of course, you want to use your dialogue to build them up, not tear them down. Even in anger and frustration, you can try to show them respect and dignity. If you don't, you're turning off the spigot of communication and creating the possibility for your relationship to dry up.

Four things allowed us to keep talking, to grow closer to each other, and to create the bond we always loved having. There are four essentials to keep the conversations going:

- Trust
- Listening
- Mutual sharing
- A win-win communication style

Implementing these four essentials will allow you to develop a relationship that will weather life's storms and create a connection that will make you the one they turn to—even when times are tough.

Talking Essential #1: Trust

Underneath all communication between my daughters and me was the trust we had in each other. We wouldn't judge one another, no matter what we said, and we wouldn't use any details later to hurt one another.

Trust is vital even in conversations that don't involve the traditional painful topics. In second grade, Andrea found herself in a social dilemma with her friends at school. For a period of time she came home distraught every day because everyone wanted to sit by her at lunch. She was completely and consistently upset because she didn't know how to handle the fact that she had only two sides and all of her friends seemed to be clamoring to be at them. This may sound like a nice problem to have, but it was a serious issue for Andrea. Making light of it would have damaged the trust she had in me to listen. So instead of laughing, teasing her, or dismissing the situation as unimportant, I listened carefully to her predicament and her feelings about it. Together we talked about possible solutions as earnestly as if we were devising a plan for world peace. As a result, I believe it built more trust between us as well as a confidence, in years to come, that she could trust me to talk to about anything.

Talking Essential #2: Listening

I'm constantly reminding myself and my clients that communication is not as much about what you say as it is about how well you hear.

Although you won't be successful every single time with your kids (I definitely wasn't), you can choose to listen more than you talk. One reason I wasn't always successful is that I *do* like to talk. Just as with most people, really listening is not easy for me. It took a lot of energy to be fully present, to watch my children's body language, to see the slight flickers in their facial features and the changing expressions in their eyes, to listen to fluctuations in their tone of voice, and to hear the choice of words they used to talk about things. Really listening and giving my total attention is a skill I learned as I became a psychotherapist, but it was equally important for me to practice it with my daughters. No, I wasn't trying to "therapize" them, but I wanted to get inside their skin. I wanted to know—even to feel—what it was like to experience what they were experiencing. Asking instead of telling can help you understand your own kids' circumstances from the inside out rather than from the outside in.

> ALTHOUGH YOU WON'T BE SUCCESSFUL EVERY SINGLE TIME WITH YOUR KIDS (I DEFINITELY WASN'T), YOU CAN CHOOSE TO LISTEN MORE THAN YOU TALK.

Listening doesn't just mean not talking. Good listening often requires asking questions and making sure you have all the information before you try to move the conversation forward. When Carol was sixteen and wanted to go to Vail with her girlfriends to ski for a couple of days, I listened to her proposal, then asked a lot of questions about how she had planned her weekend *before* I gave my opinions and concerns. Together we talked through the plans and options, and then I decided to approve. When Andrea decided she wanted to go to boarding school, I listened to her reasoning *before* I gave her mine. Together we explored the pros and cons, and she chose to stay at home. When she wanted to take a road trip with her boyfriend, my inclination was to summarily cut her off and mince her idea to a pulp. Instead, I patiently listened and asked some questions to make sure I wasn't missing any pertinent information *before* I gave her my thoughts, my reasons, and my decision, which was still a no.

But it's hard to listen well. Even when I knew what to do, I didn't always take the time to do it. Once in a while I neglected to listen, thrusting my way into my kids' lives with my own strong opinions and preconceived notions, pronouncing my decisions without listening carefully to them. Carol's adventure in the Soviet Union was one of those times. Though she was only sixteen, evidently I had decided she should have a unique summer experience by traveling far, far away. Having gathered all the information and talked with those in charge, I proceeded to make her plans and ensure her acceptance into the program. She was to join forty-two American scientists and a small group of students to spend two months in Tajikistan with a similar team of Soviets planning the first national park in their country. Only years later did she let me know how scared she'd been. In fact, she'd felt so anxious that she'd gotten physically sick boarding the plane in Denver.

Carol had realized how young she was; she'd felt alone, knowing no one else on the trip; and she'd been aware that she was looking at spending eight weeks in a tent on the other side of the world. In addition, there'd been unrest in the Soviet Union at the time she was leaving. Indeed, the country fractured and the Soviet Union fell only one week after she returned home.

Carol had had every reason to be scared, but I hadn't taken the time to give her my listening ear. In my planning mode, I'd taken the quicker, simpler route of making the decision for her rather than the longer, more circuitous one of seeking out and listening to her feelings. In retrospect, we both see that it was an amazingly significant two months in her young life, but I still feel bad that I managed to ramrod my plan through without her full agreement. Why I didn't pay more attention to her feelings in the first place, and why she didn't make sure I heard them, is something we've long since forgotten, so we'll never be able to fully understand. I only know I did the wrong thing by not listening to her.

Talking Essential #3: Mutual Sharing

Mutual sharing might be the most fun aspect of having an open line of communication. I loved engaging my kids in lots of conversations, asking questions, giving them my point of view, and guiding them through a rich exchange of thoughts and ideas—like meandering through a beautiful botanical garden, exploring this, noticing that, and enjoying the stroll just because we were together.

I promoted these kinds of conversations during our frequent car trips to Denver when they were young. Fortified with juice and snacks, we chatted about anything and everything as we cruised up and over the mountains, often in the midst of snowstorms and icy roads, sometimes in the splendor of the autumn leaves, during the wet and slushy mud season, and also throughout the summer when the glory of the mountains revealed itself in an awesome expanse of green. We had nowhere to go and nothing to interrupt, so it was the perfect time to learn more about each other through simple talk.

My favorite memories were the serious conversations I initiated about friends, God, school, honesty, drugs, alcohol, loyalty, and more. I would think in advance, *Hmmm, what would I like for us to explore together on this trip?* Carol and Andrea always knew I was waiting for the appropriate moment to shift our light chatting into a serious discussion. We were trapped together in the car for four hours, plenty of time to dig in and find out what we thought about these different topics. I loved hearing their thoughts and inspirations, because it was a way for me to really understand where they were coming from. I was almost as open about my thoughts, as if I were talking to one of my adult friends. I wanted them to know me and to know me well, and if I hadn't been open with them, they wouldn't have been able to. Mutual sharing is the best way to promote friendship. How could we build a relationship if the sharing went in only one direction?

When kids are young, sharing is a piece of cake. Carol shared how she was hurt by her friend when her friend chose to sit by someone else; I shared about my friend, who thirty years earlier, wouldn't let me jump rope with her at recess.

Andrea talked about riding her bike through town; I related how my friend Delores and I used to make peanut butter crackers, then ride our bikes down to the stream a half mile out of town and eat our crackers by the babbling water.

Carol cried as she came running in with a bump on her head from falling when she was playing; I told her about the time I fell off the bars at Melanie's house and landed flat on my back.

Carol sometimes complained that Andrea didn't want to play with her after school and that Andrea hurt Carol's feelings because she closed her door and put a sign on it saying DO NOT DISTURB. I remembered how my friends, Elaine and Becky, left me out of a play they were making up and how sad and lonely I felt.

I was careful not to offer these memories in a one-upmanship kind of way, taking the focus off of my daughters and their problems or trying to steal the limelight. I shared them to let my girls know that maybe I could understand what they were going through, because I had gone through a similar thing. Over those early years, I told them stories about my childhood to give them deeper insights into my fallibility and vulnerability and to help them know me as a person as well as a mom. It was in this gentle and enjoyable way, conversing about all kinds of things, that we became real friends, enjoying one another's company as any three friends would.

I TOLD THEM STORIES ABOUT MY CHILDHOOD TO GIVE THEM DEEPER INSIGHTS INTO MY FALLIBILITY AND VULNERABILITY AND TO HELP THEM KNOW ME AS A PERSON AS WELL AS A MOM.

Hopefully, as kids grow older, the sharing becomes more comprehensive. My kids' issues got more complicated as they aged, so I needed to respond in kind. I told them about Roger, the boy I had a huge crush on when I was a freshman in high school. When he finally asked me to the homecoming dance, I was so nervous, I stepped on his feet at the beginning of every single dance and was totally tongue-tied the entire evening. That was my first and last date with Roger. I told them about how I never felt feminine; how I was lonely on weekends because my girlfriends had dates and I was at home with my parents; how I looked like Laverne from *Laverne and Shirley,* with my rhinestone-studded, pointy-tipped glasses. I felt that sharing with them would help them to get to know me as a person with the same kind of needs, feelings, and problems they might have. I didn't want to be a mystery or a closed book. I didn't want them to be afraid of me or worried about how I would react. I wanted to be their friend.

One day several years ago I was cleaning out some boxes in storage and found an old journal I'd kept when I lived in Chicago in my early twenties. It seemed that I dated a lot of guys one particular summer and wrote rather explicitly about some of them. Together the three of us howled with laughter as I read, mostly because I had little to no memory of most of it, but my descriptions were abundant, colorful, and hilarious. Those conversations were great bonding experiences for us. Since I was willing to be vulnerable with them, it was easier for them to be vulnerable with me. Our communication became more enriched and our relationship deeper.

Of course, however good the friendship between you and your children, you have to be careful to share appropriately. While they should be able to tell you anything, that doesn't mean you should tell them everything. All parents should be able to protect their private lives. I didn't cross the line and share things like the intimate details of my marriage with their stepdad. I didn't make my kids my confidantes, tell them my burdensome troubles, or make them feel responsible or guilty for my struggles. I was still in charge, the buck stopped with me, and I made the final decisions. Overall, I was the mom, and the boundaries between us were crisp and clean.

It's a balancing act to know what to share and what to keep to yourself. A guideline for determining where to set your boundary is to think carefully about what would be useful or valuable to your children and also consider what could be detrimental to them, frighten them, or simply creep them out. For example, you wouldn't want to share the very personal things you say and do with your spouse, but you might want to share how and why you fell in love, because that can teach kids some important lessons about relationships, which will benefit them when they look for their own mates one day.

Some parents find it easy to open their past to their kids, but others have made huge mistakes that still produce guilt and shame. Even though the mistakes are painful, it may be important to share them. But if you've gone through some unsavory experiences that you'd like to blot out of your history and there's nothing beneficial your kids could learn from hearing the details, then don't give them. You can still own up to the fact that you made big blunders. Tell them how you feel about those blunders and that you've worked through them emotionally, moved beyond them, and think there would be no merit in sharing them. Your openness and honesty will let your kids know they can trust you with their own experiences.

I've heard parents respond to their children's questions by saying, "We'll talk about that when you're older," but they never have the conversation. In contrast, it might be helpful to make a list of things you want to share with your kids about your past and your experiences so you're ready when they are. You can make the list right now, no matter what ages your children are, because there are no topics that can't be talked about at any age. No topic is inappropriate. It's only the depth and detail of the conversation that needs to be tailored to meet your child's age.

With these boundaries, though, you can build a foundation of mutual sharing to base other conversations on, and you and your children can understand each other as people as well as family.

Talking Essential #4:
A Win-win Communication Style

Carol recently reminded me of this aspect of our communication: She recalled that there was never a win-lose component in our conversations. She said she didn't feel as if I thought it was necessary for me to have the last word or to make sure she knew my opinion was the right one. She said I didn't push my ideas onto her or make her feel bad or wrong if she had a different opinion. There were no winners or losers in our discussions. We just talked.

Carol gave an example of our win-win communication style from her high school days, when I often questioned her about her homework. To be honest, I would nag, nag, nag her.

"When are you going to do your homework?"

"Have you finished your homework?"

"If you watch TV, will you have time for your homework?"

To this day, I'm not sure why I targeted Carol, but I confess, she seemed to have a homework bull's-eye painted on her back. It's odd: Although she was conscientious about her schoolwork and almost always did what she was supposed to do, still I hounded her. Over time my constant questioning and doubting began to trigger her, and she would get angry.

I may be persistent, but I'm not stupid, so I could see we were going in the wrong direction. We began to talk about it, and I gave Carol permission to call me on it every time I said something about her homework that triggered her. It worked beautifully for us. It was a win-win because, not having realized what I'd been doing, I was able to change my annoying behavior, and Carol was able to realize she could be a winner in our conversations. By courageously telling me when I was nagging her, she instantly realized that I didn't have to win and that I was willing to be wrong. This was an important revelation for her and one that heightened our level of communication.

It's a big deal for both parent and child to level the playing field in conversations. You're not automatically right because you're a parent, nor are your children automatically wrong. The outcome of an argument is not preset in favor of the parent, and being right isn't the parent's default position. When you're able to let go of your ego and stand on equal ground with your kids, your reward is that you will have infinitely better communication with them. Better communication means that you're much more likely to be the person they want to *talk* to about the difficult stuff in their lives—and the person they want to *listen* to about what to do about it.

> IT'S A BIG DEAL FOR BOTH PARENT AND CHILD TO LEVEL THE PLAYING FIELD IN CONVERSATIONS. YOU'RE NOT AUTOMATICALLY RIGHT BECAUSE YOU'RE A PARENT, NOR ARE YOUR CHILDREN AUTOMATICALLY WRONG.

These four methods will help you talk to your kids and keep talking to them, whatever happens. But of course, even with good tools, there's no guarantee nothing will go wrong.

Sometimes, Nothing Seems to Work

Having good communication habits (or getting rid of bad communication habits) doesn't necessarily eliminate all the challenges that come up. Sometimes, murky situations just don't seem to have any solutions, or situations are so ambiguous that it's unclear exactly what to do.

Andrea and I encountered one of those murky situations when she was in fifth grade and had just returned from a backcountry ski trip with her school. One of the first things she told me as she peeled off her wet clothes was that one of the sixth-grade boys had smuggled a flask of vodka to the ski hut and brought it out late at night after the chaperones had snuggled into their sleeping bags. It was not unusual that she would share that type of information with me because she trusted that I wouldn't use it against her or her friends. Yet this time it was a bit different because I was on a committee of parents to review the outdoor education trips and make recommendations for the future. Andrea and I sat together and discussed whether I should report this to the committee or not, and if so, how would I safeguard her from being tagged as the one who had ratted?

We decided that I would tell the story but wouldn't name the guilty vodka smuggler, and I'd let the committee know that it was highly important that the source of the information remain anonymous. As luck would have it, the mom of the smuggler was also on the committee and surmised instantly that her son was the culprit. When she left our meeting, she went home promptly to confront her son and punish him soundly.

The next day at school Andrea was the rat, and half the kids in the middle school ridiculed and snubbed her. I felt awful. If the same situation were to pop up again, what would I do? I honestly don't know because, first and foremost, I would want to protect our relationship. My loyalties lay with her even more than with the school program. Our decision to divulge let us both down and hurt her for days. (In this particular situation, there was no real safety issue and no one would have gotten in trouble with the law, which made Andrea's and my decision to divulge even more difficult. However, many other situations can arise where there is either a legal or a safety risk. In those cases it is important to tell an authority what has happened to protect everyone involved. And it's another opportunity to discuss with your child morality, ethics, and the complexities of life.)

When Carol was a freshman in high school, she took repeated verbal beatings from a "friend." I still get mad when I think about it. Freshman girls can be like cats. Snarl, scratch, claw! My heart still dissolves in sadness when I think about how Carol practically ran out the gym door after volleyball practice, her face clutched in panic, waiting until she was safely inside the car to burst into tears. Jamie had done it again. For no apparent reason she had once more humiliated Carol in front of the girls in the locker room, saying mean things about her and calling her four-letter words.

Since I knew Jamie's mom, I called her to talk about it. She would not even mention it to Jamie and thought it best to let the two girls work it out—even if it took all four years in high school. Carol and I were left with no recourse except to talk about it between the two of us. I helped Carol see it from a different perspective: that this was a moment in time and it wouldn't go on forever. I listened to her feelings, comforted her, and let her know that it wasn't about her. Maybe Jamie was jealous of Carol for transferring into her school and being part of her circle of friends. Maybe she was afraid Carol would steal some of them away from her. We'll never know. Sometimes life sucks! At least we were able to talk about it, and I know that helped. Interestingly, they never did work it out. It eventually faded away, but they never were really good friends after that.

Recently another young girl sat in my therapy office in tears because her best friend had begun to snub and reject her. I wish I could have changed the behavior of her friend, but I could not. What I *could* do was listen attentively and compassionately, let her know that I understood her feelings, and encourage her to keep talking about it. She told me it was helpful.

Wouldn't it be great if talking solved all our problems? Unfortunately, it doesn't, but encouraging our kids to talk does let them know that we care and that we're there for them, and that can make all the difference.

You Set the Tone

Now that you know why I think communication is so important, the next step is to realize that it's under your control. Will you have good communication in your home, or will your kids feel isolated and try to find someone else to talk and listen to? It's up to you, not your kids. The adults set the tone, put the structures in place, and decide how they want to talk with the children. It's never too soon to begin thinking about the family environment you want to create. No doubt it's a lot more important than how you'll decorate the nursery.

When you have a vision for what you want your family environment to be, you can have a plan for getting there. In Stephen Covey's book *The 7 Habits of Highly Effective Families* (St. Martin's Press, 1997), he encourages parents to "begin with the end in mind." It's the same advice he gives to corporate executives and anyone who wants to be effective in any arena. In other words, people should have a goal, a direction, a reason for doing what they're doing. Parents need to create goals for their children, too, whether the goal is to create a family mission statement, to plan a special event, or to go through a single day with purpose. If you know where you want to end up, it will direct your interactions with your kids along the way. Covey says you wouldn't construct a building without first drafting a blueprint, nor would you perform a play without first writing the script, so why would you try to raise a family without creating a vision of what you want your family to be?

One way I visualize communication in a family is to think of it as being like antifreeze in the pipes of the relationship. You need to maintain a continuous flow so the pipes don't freeze up or build pressure on either end. If you understand the value of communication, you can use every opportunity to keep the conversations going—car trips, mealtimes, shoveling snow, playing with the dog, decorating the Christmas tree. Just remember, talking helps keep your family close.

Frozen pipes (bad communication) come in a variety of forms. If you don't speak to your kids at all, that tells them they're not important to you. If you scream and curse at them, that tells them that they're not valuable to you and you don't care about their feelings. But there are more subtle ways to freeze the pipes, too.

I once saw a movie about a dysfunctional family of four in which almost every sentence exchanged among the family members was just plain wrong. Parents shared inappropriately personal and intimate things about themselves with their two sons. There was a lot of yelling and fighting. People walked out on each other. No one listened to anyone else. No one was interested in anyone but him- or herself. Four-letter words cut through the air like knives. Yes, it was funny—it was a movie, after all, and the characters were witty—and it wasn't someone's real life. If it had been a real family, it wouldn't have just been pathetic;

> ONE WAY I VISUALIZE COMMUNICATION IN A FAMILY IS TO THINK OF IT AS BEING LIKE ANTIFREEZE IN THE PIPES OF THE RELATIONSHIP. YOU NEED TO MAINTAIN A CONTINUOUS FLOW SO THE PIPES DON'T FREEZE UP OR BUILD PRESSURE ON EITHER END.

it would have been tragic. Yet this does happen in real life, to real families with real hearts that get bruised and torn by what they say to one another.

The other day I was chatting with a friend who finds herself not really talking with her teenage daughter. Instead, she reprimands, demands, scolds, and punishes most of the time. (Not exactly an uncommon experience for a parent of a teenager, is it?) There's a wedge between them, and it's growing every day. Instead of an environment of warmth and support, they live in an atmosphere of suspicion, sneakiness, lying, and distrust. I encouraged my friend that it's never too late to stop and draft a new plan, or write a new script to redirect her course. I suggested that she begin by taking her daughter away for a fun weekend with just the two of them: "Allow yourself to open up and become vulnerable with your daughter," I suggested. "Share with your teen what you want and how you want to get there. Admit that you haven't used the right tactics to reach your objective, and then create a new plan with your daughter." My friend understood the value of doing this and agreed to trying, but she never really put herself into gear to do it. Unfortunately, my friend and her daughter are still struggling.

I find this to be all too common. Parents often want advice, but it can be difficult and time consuming to take the steps to put the advice into practice. Of course, it's not easy, and one weekend may not come close to turning the family ship around, but it's a start, and committing to start is often the hardest part of the journey. Remember that you're the captain of this ship, and the course you set will dictate where you end up. It may seem slow going, especially when you have to stop and plan out what you want and how to get it, but it's worth it to finally arrive where you want to be.

The Power of Negative Talking

You know that communication is the way to influence your children, teach them about who you are, and provide a guiding hand in their lives. But it can still do all that if you use it irresponsibly and negatively instead of constructively, and the damage it creates can be as important as the progress that positive communication brings. Even a small incident can cause a big effect.

In high school and long beyond, my husband, Terry, was a strong athlete: a football player, an All-American gymnast, and a dirt bike racer. He even rode bucking broncos and bulls in rodeos. Thank goodness he's given up most of that, but he still skis, hikes, and rides horses. As you might imagine, the man has great legs, but because of something his mother used to say, he used to be embarrassed by them.

Terry told me that when he was little, it was humiliating to him when his mother pointed to him and said to other people, "Look at his skinny little legs." It's taken him several decades to work through that message and feel good about wearing shorts. That's a lot of power, and she probably has no idea she ever said such a thing. Amazing how a negative message—even if it's unintentional—can inflict a sharp stab to the soul and break down a child's spirit.

I've had many clients tell me over the years about hurtful statements their parents made to them when they were children. We'll never know what those parents meant when they made these comments, but they affected decisions their children—my clients—made about their lives in adulthood. One woman got the message from her parents that she wasn't very smart, so instead of trying for a good job, she only tried for a husband who would take care of her financially, and she spent much of her adult life feeling inadequate. A young man had been convinced by his parents that he would never amount to much, so he continued to take menial jobs that never fulfilled him.

One rash comment I made to Carol still shames me, a thoughtless remark that could easily have damaged her self-image, even though we've talked about it many times. She'd just returned from a special three-month trip organized through her school. I was surprised to see that she'd gained some weight for the first time in her young life. (So what? She'd been eating different foods away from home for three months.)

For some reason, watching her show our family and a few friends a new dance she'd learned, I blurted out, "Boy, Carol, you did gain a little weight while you were gone!" I still can't believe it flew out of my mouth, and I knew the instant the words reverberated in the air around me that it was wrong, but it was too late to take them back. I've since apologized many times, and I'm still sad at what she, my dear, sweet thirteen-year-old, must have thought about herself when her mother told her that she was fat—in front of other people, no less.

If I could do it over, I might wait a few days, watching and listening, and if she expressed any concern about her weight gain, then I could help her on her terms.

You can give your children a thousand affirmations and compliments and they won't remember them, but if you fire one bullet, it will lodge in their emotional body forever. Kids of all ages are so absorbent that giving them negative messages is like spilling red wine on a new cashmere sweater. It can stain and shrink the very fabric of who they are.

I wonder if I've ever said to my daughters, "Oh, never mind. You wouldn't understand anyway." I hope not, because that statement implies that their brains aren't capable of getting it, so I might as well not waste my time trying to explain. Or what about parents who say, "Don't you ever stop and think?" or "You're so stupid!" or "Don't ask so many questions. You're driving me crazy," or "You'd better take vocational courses because you'll never go to college." Whoa!

You can see how the list could go on and on—comments that gradually pick away at a kid's belief that he or she is smart, adequate, or worthy. Then there are all the messages about "You're too . . ." fill in the blank: *fat, skinny, lazy, slow, loud, unattractive, unathletic, uninteresting.* (You wouldn't believe how many people I've had in my therapy practice who believed they weren't interesting.)

Of course, these messages affect self-esteem, marriages, and even career success as kids grow older, but they affect the relationship between parent and child immediately. No way will kids trust their hearts to a parent who speaks abusively or disrespectfully. If you want to be a part of your child's life, you must develop positive communication patterns.

In truth, I don't know of anyone who communicates perfectly. There are no perfect parents, just as there are no perfect kids. I know I've hurt my children with my words and overlooked many opportunities to make them feel better about themselves by communicating with more sensitivity and more thought. You probably can't prevent all negative talk any more than anyone else—but you must be aware of how your words affect your children and how the messages you give them shape their lives.

Crying Out for Attention

Sometimes the messages kids send are not verbal, and seem to be coming out of the blue. It might seem like you have a discipline problem with your child, rather than a communication problem. But remember the rule: When in doubt, talk it out.

When Marie came to see me some years ago, her life had fallen into shambles, and she had forgotten about the concept of communication altogether. She wanted to talk about what had happened to her daughter.

Tanya had been an adorable, active, athletic child who loved to spend time with her mom, chatting, laughing, and having fun. In the past couple of years she'd become moody, uncommunicative, and sour. Tanya would snap with anger when her mom asked her to do almost anything, and she seemed to isolate herself more and more as time went on. Marie said they had begun to argue and fight a lot, and Tanya appeared to be unhappy most of the time. Grades had dropped, interests had changed, she seemed both aggressive and depressed, and she'd gained a lot of weight.

As we continued to talk, Marie related that Tanya had begun to hang out with girls who dressed for sex, smoked in front of adults, and behaved much older than they were. More recently, she'd started going to friends' houses without telling her mom where she was. Simultaneously, she'd begun to make snide and sarcastic remarks to her mom, to walk around the house sullen and closed down, and to refuse to share anything, giving only "yes," "no," or "I dunno" answers when forced to respond.

Over the span of a few sessions with Marie, I learned a lot about why Tanya had most likely begun to react so outwardly and so negatively. The family had almost literally burst apart when Marie and her husband Harry divorced. It was a nasty divorce that never really ended. Both parents were so angry with each other that they couldn't cooperate to parent their child, and Marie confessed that she bad-mouthed Harry frequently in front of Tanya and her friends. She admitted that sometimes she'd been so angry that she refused to allow Tanya to call her dad when she wanted to and also made excuses for why Tanya couldn't visit him at the appointed times. Frustrated by his inability to make contact with his daughter, Harry had begun to drift away. Perhaps not wanting to meet with rejection, he called less and less, so he had lost his connection with his daughter.

Marie had reacted to the divorce by devoting herself to finding a new man in her life, paying increasingly less attention to Tanya and increasingly more to herself. Her social calendar was full, but it rarely included one-on-one time with Tanya. She had been so distraught, angry, and fractured by the loss of her marriage that she hadn't stopped to consider the devastation to her daughter. Her own life had taken over everything, and she'd stopped communicating with Tanya. When Marie quit conversing with her daughter, the fissure grew, gradually swallowing up Tanya as it widened and deepened.

Tanya reacted in the only way she knew how—by engaging in unacceptable behavior, hoping Mom would notice and come to her rescue. Over time Marie began to see her own part in Tanya's self-destructive behaviors and was willing to make a turnaround.

Tanya consented to coming to therapy, too. As she and I talked, she openly shared with me how she felt.

She said she'd given up sports, replacing them with girls who smoked and flirted with her mom's new boyfriend. She couldn't imagine how her mom wouldn't notice, be upset, and want to talk with her about it. She got choked up as she asked me, "Doesn't Mom care how I feel?"

She acknowledged that she was aggressive and rude to her mom, and yet her mom just blew it off as a typical adolescent phase. Even Tanya knew it's only typical to be rude to your mom when you're in trouble or bursting with pain. How could her mom not know that, she wondered? Underneath, she was dying to talk with Marie and didn't know how to get her attention any other way.

Tanya couldn't understand how she could continually sneak away and spend hours with kids her mom didn't even know, without her mom even suspecting what they might be doing and not caring enough to talk with her about it.

Tanya was gaining weight. Surely, she thought, her mom noticed that something was wrong. Tanya said that at times, she desperately wanted to cry out to her mother, "I have so much to talk to you about and you abandoned me for your more important social life, but I'm still here, dying on a vine and waiting for you to come back to me."

She told me that her mom had never even asked her how she felt when her parents split. Tanya had felt grief, pain, confusion, and fear, but Marie never talked with Tanya about any of those feelings. She felt like her mom never cared to find out what it felt like to have divorced parents, let alone parents who still fought years later. She was continually angry that Marie wouldn't let her talk with her dad because she missed him, and she was hurt and furious that her mom opted for a new boyfriend instead of spending time with her. In fact, she'd always thought the divorce was *her* fault because she was the one left behind by both of them. And she was mad that Marie bad-mouthed her dad in front of her. It hurt her so deeply because she still loved him and realized she was a part of him. In addition, it embarrassed Tanya when her mom talked like that in front of Tanya's friends.

With tears in her eyes, Tanya poured out to me, "Why won't she talk to me like she used to? It makes me feel unimportant and worthless. It feels like I'm falling into a deep, dark hole. I'm sad and depressed, and I don't understand any of it." Then she hardened a little as she added that if her mom wouldn't come toward her soon, it would be too late, and she wouldn't want to talk to her at all.

Little by little, Tanya and her mom began to talk with one

another again. At first they needed help having a conversation even about simple subjects, because Tanya had lost her trust in her mom and was reluctant to tell her anything. If she had shared something of value, and her mom had scorned it or ignored it, it would have torn Tanya's heart to shreds, so the mending went very slowly. They had to learn to reconnect. Indeed, repairing tattered communication habits can be a long process, requiring a great deal of patience and determination, yet it's the best way I know to get the relationship back on track.

> REPAIRING TATTERED COMMUNICATION HABITS CAN BE A LONG PROCESS, REQUIRING A GREAT DEAL OF PATIENCE AND DETERMINATION, YET IT'S THE BEST WAY I KNOW TO GET THE RELATIONSHIP BACK ON TRACK.

Good communication doesn't automatically solve all the problems—nothing can. It doesn't necessarily prevent kids from doing things their own way and paying for the consequences, but even then, talking helps. When we lose our communication, we lose our connection and our relationship and find ourselves alone and floundering in an unforgiving world. It should always be our goal, as parents and stepparents, to give our children the gift of communication to build and fortify the relationship. It may be the greatest gift we can give our kids. Communication keeps us connected.

Dear Carol and Andrea,

I can't wait until each of you has kids of your own. You're going to be bowled over by how much you love your adorable and precious infant. Very soon you'll begin to differentiate the cries of hunger from those of being sleepy or having a messy bottom—the cries of wanting to be held from those of pain and discomfort.

Then one day you'll discern a slightly different tone, one that seems to wail out, "I'm gonna bawl and whine and complain until you do what I want. I'll drive you crazy until you do it my way!"

That's the day the notion of discipline will first waft through your brain, and you'll realize you'd better come up with a plan for raising your child. And that's the day I'll be glad I'm the grandma and not the mom!

I love you bushels and nightgowns,

Mom

CHAPTER 3

Boil It Down to the Basics:

Approaching Discipline Through Relationship

O N THE FRONT END OF PARENTHOOD, most of us don't know what to do. On the back end, we wipe our brows with relief when it's over. Along the way, we slowly, gradually learn a few things about discipline. We botch it plenty of times, and when we find something that works, we pray that it'll be just as effective the next time. Our family learned a few things about discipline the hard way when we invited a foster child into our home. It was a struggle to find something that worked.

Isn't Love Enough?

We didn't know it right away, but the day the front door opened and our foster child, Melody, walked in was the day our family began a rip-roarin' roller-coaster ride. Carol and Andrea were both quite young, about six and eight, when my ex-husband and I (still married at the time) decided to take in a seventeen-year-old foster daughter. How magnanimous we felt! We had no idea what we were in for, and we were in over our heads. Melody came from a single-parent home with several siblings, all from different fathers. Her mom used drugs regularly and was constantly in trouble with the law for her backyard pot garden. Mom was neither present nor caring with the children. Since Melody had grown up neglected, she had learned to be streetwise and take care of herself as best she could. Her social worker told us there were no particular problems, that all Melody needed was stability, warmth, and a family she could count on. The social services representatives must have been on another planet when they interviewed Melody and her mom, but we were too naïve to see the reality and predict the future.

IF THERE'S NO WELL-DEVELOPED, UNDERLYING RELATIONSHIP BETWEEN PARENTS AND KIDS, THEN TRYING TO APPLY DISCIPLINE IS LIKE HOLDING UP A HOUSE BUILT ON A FOUNDATION OF SAND.

With great enthusiasm we swooped in and scooped up our new daughter. We gave her the spare bedroom to arrange and decorate as she wanted. She had her own phone, home-cooked breakfasts and dinners, allowance money in her pocket, and a ready-made loving family. In some ways, she probably thought she had died and gone to heaven.

What occurred over the next nine months made clear to me that a parent's control over his or her children is not real. It is a fragile illusion at best. If there's no well-developed, underlying relationship between parents and kids, then trying to apply discipline is like holding up a house built on a foundation of sand. The whole family structure crumbles. As soon as you repair one section, another falls down. You spend a lot of time frantically whizzing from one segment to the other, propping up the walls and shoring up the cracks. You live in dread of the next catastrophe, never exactly knowing when or where it will occur—only that it *will* occur. It's a helpless feeling, one that really shakes your confidence in yourself. There's little peace and even less enjoyment. The whole experience of parenting turns into a nightmare.

We were incredibly ignorant to believe that we could jump into the middle of Melody's life with no preparation, training, or support system behind us. I firmly believed that developing a deep and trusting relationship with my own children from their early childhood days would be the basis of our whole family structure. In fact, I had already spoken with them about the inadequacy of power and authority as a basis for family interaction. I knew discipline had to be rooted in mutual trust and respect as well as shared family values and family culture. I'm not sure why I suddenly threw all that out the window and opted for the philosophy that if we were just kind and loving, it would make up for the first seventeen years of Melody's life. If we just started in the now, I foolishly thought, we could pretend her early years of no training, no guidance, no consistency, no communication, no stability, no caring, and no dependable relationship wouldn't matter. Well, they *do* matter.

The first few weeks with our new foster daughter were sweet, and we felt like heroes. Melody was fun and happy, bubbly and excited to be with us. She joined right in, participating in our lively family conversations, and she loved playing with Carol and Andrea. We thought we were now the perfect little family of five and that parenting a teenager was a piece of cake. Then, after the honeymoon period, things began to decline. Melody wasn't quite as cooperative or helpful and began to separate herself from us to enclose herself in her room and talk on the phone with her friends.

In retrospect, I wonder why we expected her to fit in with us. She had never learned to communicate or to bond with her own family—any family. How could we have expected her to know how to do that with us?

We approached discipline with common sense and reason, the same way I expected to do it with my own kids. Since we hadn't developed a history with Melody, nor assimilated her into our family culture, the common sense and reason belonged only to us. It didn't seem to overlap into any world she had ever lived in. As she began to default to her early survival training, we became ships passing in the night.

Although we established rules and set boundaries, Melody blew them off. At first I didn't realize what was happening. Then I began to have visions dancing through my head, and they were not visions of sugarplums. They were visions of that afternoon several years before in our kitchen in front of the stove when I first talked with my daughters about the idea of building a relationship with them. It seemed that my theory was proving itself. Its core was even clearer to me now: control is, indeed, a mirage.

Let me state it again: Parental control exists only if your child gives it to you. Our experience with Melody is an example of the key element in discipline, especially in the teen years: Your child grants you the authority to impose discipline because of the long-standing, trusting relationship you share. Because Melody didn't give it to us, we were in for a rough ride.

Melody stayed out all night at her boyfriend's house; she made many long-distance phone calls, which we had not given her permission to make; and we were sure she stole money from our wallets even though she denied it. The succeeding months became more tense as we quickly installed more rules, which Melody naturally didn't want to follow.

PARENTAL CONTROL EXISTS ONLY IF YOUR CHILD GIVES IT TO YOU.

We set up consequences, such as: *In the real world, if you can't pay your phone bill, your phone gets disconnected. From now on, your phone has been disconnected—you have no phone privileges.* But who wants to be the phone police lurking about the house monitoring whether Melody's lifting the receiver off the hook? She still needs lunch money, but who's to determine if she's eating a friend's lunch and using her money to buy cigarettes and beer? If she's disobeyed her curfew, a logical consequence is to ground her, but now we have to stay home to check on her—and how do we know she doesn't sneak out after we're asleep? What a mess!

We had developed a power struggle. I've often told my clients in therapy to avoid power struggles with their kids at all costs. A parent might win a single battle, but tomorrow will come and the overall war will surely have a lose-lose outcome. Without a mutually respectful relationship, parenting is a much bigger challenge.

We didn't know what to do next. Although we had compassion for Melody, we realized that what she'd been through in her life was more than we could address successfully in our home. She had no boundaries, no internal controls, no background of rules with consequences, and no experience of family life. During her earlier years of fending for herself, she'd developed some ways of coping with the world that made it very difficult for her to be a part of our family.

We continued to try with her, but Melody simply defied us. The power struggle waged on and eventually escalated to the point of no return. One afternoon, rebelliously unwilling to abide by our rules, she became physically violent. With four-letter words roaring out of her mouth and all four limbs kicking and flailing, she broke the banister on the stairway and punched a hole in the wall. Frightened, we called the police, who took her, still raging, from our home. Of course, we cried when she was gone. We were sad and relieved and feeling defeated by our failure to get through to her. I'm sure she shed tears, too, but by then it was too late for any of us to start over.

Melody was placed in a group home where rules were rigidly set and enforced by people trained to handle difficult kids, and where defiance was dealt with by the legal system. The kind of training and regimen they used to help kids get back on track lies beyond the normal scope of a family and would be almost impossible to carry out at home. Melody was fortunate to be able to get this kind of training, given her history of parental neglect and abuse.

We visited her at the group home, sent her gifts from time to time, attended her high school graduation, and communicated with her as she went out to find her place in the world. Reports I heard about Melody years later were that she still lied to people when it was convenient and stole from those who were generous to her. She continued to have promiscuous relationships with men and clung to them dependently as her mother had modeled for her.

Now I've lost track of Melody, and my heart is still saddened by the hardship of her life. Her story confirms for me the importance of building a relationship with your kids as early as possible and growing it for a lifetime. Young people need a relationship that is grounding for them and that provides stability they can count on. They need warmth, respect, communication, and trust.

Trying to discipline from the premise of control doesn't work well because you simply cannot maintain control as the child grows older. Why not start from a more effective position in the first place? Build a relationship first so you and your child understand, trust, and respect each other. As parents, we have a much better chance of helping our kids become reliable young people and good citizens if we work *with* them instead of opposing or commanding them.

How to Make It Work

Creating the environment in which you can apply discipline is no easy task, and a lot depends on your perspective. With my girls, I figured out that it's easier to suggest than to demand, and it works better to advise than to require. It's a steep, tough climb if you don't operate as a team and continue to build a lot of trust and respect with each other as you go. It helps to put discipline in the context of four specific goals, as we did in our household. Following were our four discipline goals:

- Protecting
- Teaching
- Helping them set internal limits
- Encouraging them to think for themselves

If you practice these goals, you will increase the odds that your children will grow up to be reliable, responsible, and independent adults.

Discipline Goal #1: Protecting

When Carol and Andrea were very young, it was important to give them some strict rules. *Don't stick the fork into the electrical outlet. Don't run into the street. Don't stand at the edge of the cliff.* These restrictions did not reflect a moral code or an ethic of a healthy lifestyle. They simply ensured their physical safety. Much of my early parenting was instilling into my daughters those natural laws of the universe. Since there's no gray area, the rules are black and white. It's not okay to stick the fork halfway into the plug. You can't run halfway into the street and still be safe. It's all or nothing.

As they grew beyond childhood, my daughters internalized these natural laws, but even when they became teenagers, there were things from which they needed to be protected. I wanted to implant in their brains that they are neither invincible nor immortal. Driving too fast and recklessly can cause accidents and deaths. Using drugs, especially early and frequently, can cause addiction. Hanging around troubled kids can influence them negatively. Because the risk of *not* protecting them was so great and the cost of them falling into these dangerous crevices was too high, I set boundaries, established rules, and created consequences for disobeying. I loved them and wanted to protect them.

Since toddlers and very young children don't understand logic and consequences, it's sometimes necessary to get their attention immediately to protect them from harm. A firm voice may be enough. It shouldn't sound angry or harsh, but it's okay to let them know when their behavior upsets you. Most kids respond to a firm voice—especially if you save it for the times that really matter. They sense your displeasure, and because the thing they want to do most is to please you, they're likely to correct their misbehavior to get back into your good graces.

As your children get older, you rely more on the relationship you've already established to talk with them in interactive discussions about the hazards of life and how to protect themselves. You can't lecture or preach, or they will tune you out. This is when you'll be glad you've already begun to share with them about your own life and your experiences so they know your concerns are practical and rooted in real-life events.

You can also tell your children how you feel: "When you ride your bike across the intersection without looking, it frightens me because I'm afraid you'll get hit by a car." Kids need to learn that there's a world out there beyond themselves and their behaviors have an emotional impact on those around them.

> KIDS NEED TO LEARN THAT THERE'S A WORLD OUT THERE BEYOND THEMSELVES AND THEIR BEHAVIORS HAVE AN EMOTIONAL IMPACT ON THOSE AROUND THEM.

When Carol started driving with her permit, she developed the habit of rolling through stop signs. Here's what I said (in a loud, angry voice with two of her friends in the backseat): "Carol, if you don't learn to come to a full stop, I will not ever allow you to drive the car by yourself! And I don't care what you think."

In football, they'd call that a fumble.

Here's what I should have said (in a firm voice, alone with just her): "Carol, when you roll through the intersection, I'm very frightened to be in the car with you. I'm concerned that you don't understand the dangers involved in driving and you haven't learned enough responsibility to drive alone. Even when you get your license I'm not going to allow you to drive by yourself until you've proven to me that you're a responsible driver. And I will do my best to help you learn to be a very good driver."

How I actually reprimanded her humiliated her in front of her friends and didn't honor our relationship. How I *should* have handled it would have shown her respect and built more trust in me.

Discipline Goal #2: Teaching

Instructing children in how the world works and how they can succeed within it is a more challenging disciplinary goal. As children grow older, parenting gets trickier because it begins to enter the realm of morals, standards, and ethics. Respect for self and others, how to treat family and friends, honesty, integrity, and responsibility are the issues around which discipline revolves. Now the relationship becomes especially important, because it allows you to talk in greater depth about the lessons and the objectives.

With my own daughters we had plenty of discussions intended to help them learn to get along better in the world both as youngsters and when they got older. We talked about the importance of sharing their toys, not slapping, yelling, or biting, getting organized, managing their time, and doing household chores. As we talked, I also explained *why* they needed to abide by those standards. And at the end of the talking, there was a line they couldn't cross. They couldn't just talk with me and then get their way. When I said no, it meant no. This is a key part of teaching discipline—without it, none of your well-meaning discussions are likely to work.

As an adult, Andrea once lived next to neighbors who had a three-year-old child who she could often hear screaming through the wall of her apartment. The parents told Andrea that they didn't believe in discipline, per se, and preferred talking and reasoning with their child about everything—from what he chose to eat for dinner to how he behaved and when he'd go to bed at night.

It's an interesting idea and valid up to a point, but they'd forgotten that a toddler has quite limited reasoning capacity. Instead of the parents teaching their child appropriate behaviors, the child taught his parents to put up with his unruliness.

Now, at age six, this child hits his little friends without restraint and has already been suspended from school for unacceptable behavior. It seems that his parents didn't create a line he couldn't cross, and now the child is paying a price for his own narcissistic whims.

How can children learn boundaries and socially acceptable behavior if parents don't teach them? A stern no is a good place to start with a small child, followed by a short, succinct explanation. You demonstrate that behaviors *do* have consequences. Authority is a reality in our world, and even small children need to learn to obey reasonable requests, instructions, and rules. "No! It hurts Mommy when you poke me in the eye," you might begin. Then you follow up: "Please don't ever do that again." If children repeat the behavior, it's appropriate to move to a more serious measure. An immediate time-out helps to connect their misconduct to the consequence and teach them better behavior.

As for spanking, the pendulum seems to swing from one generation to another between accepting it as appropriate and rejecting it altogether. Today, it's more at the "not appropriate" end, but if you find yourself resorting to a quick swat, don't reprimand yourself or feel guilty. Just remember, the value of a swat is to get young children's attention about their misbehavior, not to hurt them. When they grow old enough to reason with, spanking is probably the least effective way to teach them a lesson because they're so focused on the fear of the imminent swat that they're incapable of hearing anything you say.

In any kind of discipline, leave your anger behind. Imposing discipline out of anger gives your children the message that they get punished when you get angry rather than when they misbehave. Tie the discipline to the behavior rather than to your feelings about it. You can *get* angry, you *can* express your anger, but wait until you've calmed down before you take action. It may take you five seconds or five minutes to release your steam, but take the time. Otherwise, your children may become afraid of you and your feelings because you appear unpredictable and out of control—the opposite of being worthy of your child's trust and respect.

IN ANY KIND OF DISCIPLINE, LEAVE YOUR ANGER BEHIND.

The younger the child, the more immediate a disciplinary action needs to be so that the child connects the infraction with the consequence. If you need to let a small misbehavior slip by because you're too angry to respond in time, remember you will have the opportunity to respond the next time. Be sure to separate your children from their behavior. Their behavior can be bad, but children are *not* bad, and letting them know that makes it much easier for them to correct the behavior.

Restricting privileges can teach kids powerful lessons. When you take away privileges—like a favorite activity or a playtime—try to do it with caring and compassion, to protect the concept that you are on the same team with them. "I'm sorry, Carol, that you didn't get your room cleaned up. Now you won't be able to watch your favorite TV program. I hope you'll get it done by tomorrow so we can watch it together."

Of course, the preferable way of disciplining is always reinforcing good behavior—like giving stickers or coins toward buying something special. Kids of every age love added privileges, and the most nurturing of all is giving regular, honest, and specific praise for what they've done well. I don't know anyone who doesn't bask in the warmth of positive affirmations, which all parents should be giving to kids on a constant basis.

I tried to give my girls choices when I could because making their own decisions built self-esteem and taught them to express their opinions and preferences. Sometimes this means choosing your battles. When Andrea was about three, she insisted on wearing dresses every day—actually the same dress every day. From my point of view, pants would have been a more logical option, considering we live in snow country, but as long as we kept her warm, it wasn't really an important issue. Ultimately, her dad and I insisted on some warm leggings and decided to let her wear whatever she wanted.

As my girls grew older, I really liked the idea of negotiation and compromise because I thought it would prepare them for the real world. Andrea was about ten when she fell into the habit of not making her bed. No matter how I scolded or hounded her, her bed remained a tousled mess. One day when she was playing in her room, I invited myself in and plopped down on her jumbled comforter. "What's the deal with this messy bed?" I asked, finally having decided that talking with her might produce better effects than reprimanding her. As we conversed, she told me that she wanted to have a bedroom that was different from everyone else's. An ordinary room was tidy and neat, but she didn't want what was ordinary, so leaving her bed unmade was her attempt to create something out of the ordinary. Her reasoning made me smile.

We continued to talk. I understood Andrea's desire for the uncommon, but I also wanted her to appreciate that I wasn't keen on a messy room. As we negotiated back and forth, we came to a terrific compromise. I would allow her to plaster her entire ceiling with posters, which would fulfill her need for the unusual, and she would, in turn, make her bed. We both loved her newly wallpapered ceiling, and she made her bed as regularly as clockwork from then on. I think each of us learned a good lesson. I learned that compromise is a wonderful tactic in disciplinary issues, and she learned that her mom could be reasonable and fair.

> I LEARNED THAT COMPROMISE IS A WONDERFUL TACTIC IN DISCIPLINARY ISSUES, AND SHE LEARNED THAT HER MOM COULD BE REASONABLE AND FAIR.

One of the most important lessons I learned along the way was that discipline should always be logical. Makes sense, doesn't it? Otherwise, you teach a child that the world is chaotic and that consequences are capricious. Some years ago, Andrea told me of an odd and confusing incident when she was spending the weekend with a friend who had a fourteen-year-old sister, Sara. According to Andrea, Sara asked her dad if she could go to an afternoon party the next day with some kids from her school. Her dad replied that if she did her household chores before leaving and found a ride both to and from the party, she could go. As Andrea was listening to the exchange, she was reasoning out the requirements in her own older, more mature mind. (She was about eighteen at the time.) Doing the chores made sense because Sara had household responsibilities she had to fulfill before she could play. Andrea assumed both parents would be gone during the time of the party, thus necessitating Sara getting a ride both ways.

The next day rolled around and party time neared. Sara came excitedly to her dad, who was reading the paper in the living room, and exclaimed, "I've done my chores and I have a ride home, but I couldn't find anyone to drive me to the party." Her dad looked up from the paper and stated matter-of-factly, "Well, then I guess you can't go."

Sara's excitement changed instantly to dejection, then to protest. "But, Dad! I don't think that's fair! I did everything I could!" As her dad summarily dismissed her, she slowly turned and walked downheartedly out of the room.

Andrea's question to me was, "Why wouldn't he let her go simply because she couldn't find a ride? He could have just driven her himself. He punished her for something that was out of her control. What was the purpose of his discipline?"

I had no idea then, and I still don't understand it. I was familiar with the dynamics of the family, though, so I can guess. Perhaps he was disciplining to prove he was the boss. Since his demands depended on other people rather than Sara, he was setting her up for failure under the guise of disciplining her. She probably saw the lack of logic in his discipline. He was also cranking into place for Sara the idea that discipline is somewhat capricious, and that she couldn't trust her dad to be reasonable. Wrong lesson to teach! Because he didn't give her a chance to express her feelings, she was learning that she couldn't talk to her dad. Another wrong lesson to teach. Instead of strengthening the concept of being on the same team, he was gradually pushing her away from him.

If you're a parent of children who haven't yet reached adolescence, it's wise to constantly remind yourself that if you lose your tight relationship with them now, it will be much harder as those teenage years chug along. By all means, now is the time to cement that relationship into place and make sure you're communicating well.

My daughters weren't perfect little angels, but they didn't rebel. I think it's because we didn't have many official rules and even fewer punishments. Since no new learning can take place when a person is in stress mode, talking and brainstorming seemed like a better strategy than punishing. How can you get your homework done and still have time to watch your favorite TV programs? How can you pick up your clothes in your room without feeling like a maid? How can you get your chores done without cutting into your playtime with friends? Instead of asking them to do something and then sitting back and waiting for them to fail, I tried to help my daughters succeed by reminding them, working with them on their schedule, and even pitching in to help at times. Instead of *having* to please me, they *wanted* to please me, because we were in it together.

Discipline Goal #3: Helping Them Set Internal Limits

This goal is closely linked with the goal of teaching, but it has a specific focus on helping kids learn the principle of internalizing their own boundaries. With effective parental discipline, when you're not around, your kids can discipline themselves.

One time I asked my girls to think about those "choose your own adventure" novels they used to read, where the plot would go so far, and then they could choose to turn to page thirty-seven or page sixty-four or page one hundred to continue the story. Depending on which page they chose, the plot flipped in an entirely different direction with an entirely different outcome. I considered those page choices to be analogous to pivotal points in their lives.

WITH EFFECTIVE PARENTAL DISCIPLINE, WHEN YOU'RE NOT AROUND, YOUR KIDS CAN DISCIPLINE THEMSELVES.

Choosing to cave in and smoke pot at a party was like turning to page thirty-seven. The story would continue by pointing them toward more drugs, hanging out with kids who used drugs, and gradually becoming more accustomed to a life wrapped around alcohol and drugs.

Choosing to go out for sports was like turning to page sixty-four. Their story would proceed with daily practices with their teammates, weekends at games, and a social life with the athletes in school.

Beginning to shoplift was like turning to page one hundred. If they got away with it the first time, they would be more apt to try again, and their lives could start moving toward the sneaky, the undercover, and the illegal.

I used to tell each of my daughters that every day was like writing another page in the history of her life, and I asked both of them to be alert to the decisions they were making. They each formulated another small piece of who they were becoming.

When Carol and Andrea were both still in high school, Terry and I went away for the weekend and left them to take care of themselves. After we returned home, they told us that they had discussed having a party while we were gone. They'd talked about what a good party house we had and how tons of kids would have come. Then they'd thought again. The house, most assuredly, would have been trashed, and I would have gotten upset. They told me that they respected me too much to violate our trust in each other. The fun of that one night would not have compensated for what we would have lost between us. It wouldn't have been worth it, so they'd both decided against the party. They called upon their internal limits.

I must admit that this good behavior was counterbalanced another time when Terry and I were away for a few days and left the girls by themselves. We went over all the rules and the dos and don'ts before we left and felt comfortable to be gone. When we returned home they told us, with big grins on their faces, that they'd disobeyed all the rules: They'd stayed out later than we'd specified; they hadn't gone to bed at the designated times; and they'd eaten ice cream for dinner. Oh, well— they weren't perfect, but that wasn't so bad, either, and at least they told us about it!

If you don't blow up at your kids or rush to punish them, you earn the privilege of talking with them. They'll be willing to tell you what they were thinking, how they viewed the situation, and what caused them to decide what they did. And you have the opportunity to share your experience and wisdom and teach them a better way.

Discipline Goal #4: Encouraging Them to Think for Themselves

Helping kids learn to think for themselves is another layer deeper than helping them set their internal boundaries, and it comes gradually as they grow older and more mature. Being able to apply the lessons you've taught them about how to treat others and how to behave in situations you're all familiar with—even when you're not there—is important. But deciding how to behave on the spur of the moment—in an entirely new situation—requires independence and confidence. This goal comes straight from my dad. One of the gifts he gave me when I was a kid was the challenge to think for myself. He used to say, "Stand on your own two feet. Don't just follow the crowd. Decide for yourself what you want to do and then be responsible for your choices."

When I became a parent, I remembered this important message and decided I wanted to reinforce it with my daughters. When they were young, I tried to give them many opportunities to make decisions on their own, hoping that would teach them to be independent thinkers. But the test really comes when they're older and spend more time on their own and with friends. When Andrea was fourteen, she began to have experiences at parties where kids dipped, smoked pot, drank, and smoked cigarettes. She had made a firm decision to abstain from all of these. At first kids asked her to join in, but she declined with confidence. She was the only one who didn't partake. She didn't follow the crowd. Thinking back, she recalls that it took real courage the first couple of times to stand solid because, at the beginning, she didn't know what the peer pressure might be. But after that, no one ever cajoled her or made fun of her. She was resolute and no one bothered her or tried to beat her down. In fact, some of the kids loved that she was always the sober one, and when she was older, they relied on her to be the designated driver. A couple of her friends even made her a mixed tape entitled "The Designated Driver Mix."

Of course, I was never present when these events occurred and only heard about them after the fact. That's the point. You won't be there either when your kids have to make a spur-of-the-moment decision. That's when you'll be glad, as I was, that your son has learned to stand on his own two feet, that your daughter has learned to think for herself.

Of course, teaching your children to think for themselves means they may not always see eye to eye with you, and that can hurt. When Carol and Andrea were both teenagers, I once lamented to Terry how they seemed to be diverting off on their own pathways. They already had a different connection with God than I did; their political views were beginning to diverge from mine; their perspective on the world, the environment, technology, life, and the future were taking separate turns from mine. I was kind of sad because, since I felt I'd been understanding and loving, I had assumed they would naturally see things my way when they grew older. I was beginning to feel betrayed. I'd given them my heart and soul, but they didn't always decide the way I would have decided.

I sniveled and said, "Why don't they do what I taught them?"

Terry's response was quick. "They're doing exactly what you taught them. You taught them to evaluate and think for themselves."

He had a point. I had never *really* wanted them to blindly obey or become little clones of me. When they were young girls, I wanted to teach them to think for themselves and to make wise and responsible decisions that would take them where they wanted to go in their lives. To accomplish that, I didn't need to be a general, constantly imposing rules, exerting my authority and expecting them to obey like recruits in boot camp. I did need to talk with them, teach them, counsel them. I loved watching them think independently and plot their own courses, and I loved the young women they were becoming.

To help your kids develop the skills of independent thinking, begin early. Start when they're still toddlers, allowing them to make small decisions that have only small consequences. Even if their choices are not ideal, no harm is done, and your children will begin to learn *how* to choose. Reinforce their good choices and discuss the ones that didn't turn out so well, so they have the opportunity to learn from their mistakes. As they grow older, invite them to participate in family decision making and ask them to share their thinking process. As you talk with them about your own standards, your own moral and ethical dilemmas surrounding the behaviors you do and decisions you make, they will internalize these standards for themselves. Unconsciously, they'll be much more likely to call upon these standards when you're not around. And if you can start only when your children are older, don't despair. The same principles apply to older kids as well. If you practice patience and understanding, it's never too late to help them become independent thinkers.

Children will always someday learn to think for themselves, but if you help them with this process, you can watch as their minds, personalities, and views on the world develop. You'll be there to see the lovely surprises and the tough choices where they choose the best path. And you'll know that they have the character and reasoning abilities to do better than just following the crowd, even if you're not around.

Sometimes the idea of imposing discipline can seem overwhelming. But it doesn't have to be if you keep it simple and boil it down to the basics. First, build a strong, positive relationship as the umbrella for every disciplinary action you take. If the discipline would hurt the relationship, don't use it. If you don't have an opportunity to talk about the discipline, it's useless. If you can't apply discipline in a way that is respectful to your children, it will be harmful. And if the discipline does not help protect or teach your children, or help them set internal limits or think for themselves, what is the point?

> SOMETIMES THE IDEA OF IMPOSING DISCIPLINE CAN SEEM OVERWHELMING. BUT IT DOESN'T HAVE TO BE IF YOU KEEP IT SIMPLE AND BOIL IT DOWN TO THE BASICS.

Here's the reality. When your kids are young, they do, indeed, obey out of blind submission. You ask them to do something and they jump to it—or not—and then there are consequences. You're big; they're little. You're in charge. But when they get older, they figure it out. They realize that you simply can't walk by their side every single minute, whispering instructions in their ears, forcing them to do it your way. There's just no way you can have total control over your kids. There's no guarantee that they'll do what you want them to do when they're out of your sight—and sometimes not even when they're in the room with you!

You need something better than a temporary illusion of power and control. To effectively discipline your kids, you need a strong relationship with them. Let's face it: Your kids grant you permission to have authority over them. They give you permission to discipline them. Why do they do that? Because they trust and respect you. Because you have proven to them through the constancy of your relationship with them over the years that you care about them, that you are fair, that you are not frivolous or capricious with them. Even though they may get temporarily angry or disappointed with you, they allow you to discipline them. If you don't have that permission, discipline becomes a nightmare filled with disobedience, rebellion, power struggles, chaos, and pain. It's your connection with your kids that makes it work—even in the tough times.

Moderation and the Middle Way

When I was growing up, it seemed like the wildest kids, the ones who were always pushing the boundaries and getting into trouble, came from either the strictest families or the most permissive ones.

The research on parenting confirms that kids can get out of control in unhealthy ways at either extreme. You can be cool, you can be friends with your kids, but you have to find a way to live in the balance between being too loose and indulgent on one end and too harsh and punitive on the other.

While working on my dissertation, I read a lot of books and articles about the field of management and leadership. The literature described various styles of leadership in organizations, and I found strong correlations to parenting styles in a home. Two distinctly different types of leadership caught my eye. In the first one, leaders treat their employees as if they never have to see them again, as if each interaction is a single episode or event. It's as if there will be no tomorrow, so the leader is a little bit like a football player: knock 'em down and run for the goalposts, regardless of who's in the way. This approach may seem too dramatic to be part of our modern world, but there are still plenty of managers and employees who don't consider the negative effects of their control or the feelings of the people who work for them.

TO EFFECTIVELY DISCIPLINE YOUR KIDS, YOU NEED A STRONG RELATIONSHIP WITH THEM. LET'S FACE IT: YOUR KIDS GRANT YOU PERMISSION TO HAVE AUTHORITY OVER THEM.

In the second type, the leaders believe it's important to set the stage for positive, continuous interaction. They know their future success depends on how they treat people now, so they build a team by discussing issues with them, respecting their ideas, including them in problem solving, and encouraging participation in decision making. If you translate this to family dynamics, you can imagine the difficulties for kids growing up in the first scenario and the advantages for kids growing up in the second one.

One patient of mine, Conrad, had grown up with parents who used the gruff, dictatorial, run-over-their-morale approach. No wonder he'd been a rebellious kid! As an adult, he came to me for therapy, finally having realized how much of his life he'd wasted being angry and choosing behaviors simply because they offended, hurt, or enraged his parents.

When Conrad was a teen, his dad rarely engaged him in discussions about his life or his activities. Instead, he callously dictated policy. Discipline consisted of telling Conrad what he couldn't do and punishing him without any questions or conversation when he disobeyed. This punitive, severe parenting style lacked warmth, prevented dialogue, and never taught him to think wisely about his choices.

By the time Conrad became an adult, he had unintentionally created a deep-rooted pattern of offensive behaviors that were detrimental to his own success in life—with friends, in relationships, and at his job. He had become a surly, offensive guy, quick to blow his top and to be insensitive to other people. In therapy he came to understand that he'd never really made decisions in his own interests; he'd only made them against his parents. It took a lot of work to dig down inside and scrape out the anger that had gummed up Conrad's decision-making apparatus. What an unfortunate legacy his parents had left him.

How you discipline your kids clearly has a huge impact on their behavior. For instance, it can predict how likely they are to use drugs. In their book *Raising Self-Reliant Children in a Self-Indulgent World* (in 2000, Random House released a fully revised and updated tenth-anniversary edition), H. Stephen Glenn and Jane Nelsen concluded that several parenting styles can raise the risk of drug usage. Some parents are overly permissive, giving kids too much autonomy and too little structure. Others are too strict and controlling, imposing excessive power and authority. Still others are downright hostile, demonstrated through being neglectful, uncaring, or disrespectful. If kids have any one of these kinds of parents, they're at higher risk for using drugs.

Excessively permissive parenting has effects beyond drug use, too. My client Lisa was a case in point. When she and her mom came to see me for counseling, it was clear that twenty-two-year-old Lisa had long ruled the household. She'd grown up with no structure, no parameters, and no guidance, and "permissive" was her mom's middle name.

Lisa had done anything she wanted from the moment she was old enough to think it up, and Mom, in her desire to be hip and cool, never said no. Lisa had started doing drugs when she was twelve, and she and her mom talked about it in my office as though they were discussing lemonade. Aside from bad grades at school, the drugs had gotten Lisa into unhealthy relationships with much older boys and into two serious car accidents. But none of these crises was enough to make Mom put her foot down and try to change the patterns she and her daughter were setting. Mom was desperate to be Lisa's friend but seemed to have misunderstood that she could have been a much better friend if she had embraced her role as parent, setting boundaries and consequences. If only Mom had communicated with Lisa about ethical and moral standards. If only they had talked about right and wrong. If only they had explored Lisa's goals for her life and how to reach them.

By the time they came to my office, Lisa had already set the course of her life and was old enough to be independent. Her mom was not pleased, but it was too late to gain control. She whined about how Lisa was making the wrong decisions, but Lisa had already been on her own for so long that she paid no attention to her mom. Mom had lost the opportunity to help her daughter create internal boundaries that would lead to her success.

The way we approach discipline with our kids sets the stage for how they feel about themselves and interact with the world around them. When parents are either too punitive and inflexible or too permissive and tolerant, kids act out. They're much more likely to thrive as responsible young adults when parents treat their kids with respect and consistent, loving guidance.

Over the years in my therapy practice, I've had parents who agreed in principle to "the middle way" but didn't know how to apply the ideas. It's often difficult to maintain a middle ground—a balance between being too inflexible and too permissive. If you're on the punitive end, you may find yourself overreacting and thinking of ways to get the upper hand—not to solve a problem or resolve an issue, but to make sure your child does it *your* way in *your* timing.

On the permissive end, some parents are so busy trying to be friends with their kids that they don't take their misbehaviors seriously. Some turn their heads and chalk up the misconducts to normal childhood or teenage behavior, hoping they'll grow out of it. Indeed, they will grow beyond the present behavior, but without your guidance, the risk is greater that your kids will not grow up to be responsible and reliable.

If you lose the middle way, on either end of the spectrum, talk with your child. Explain to him how you've gotten off track and how you want to get back on. Be firm but be open to conversation and to hearing what your child has to say. The longer you've been off the middle way, the longer it may take to get back on, but on some level, your child will respect you for caring enough to want to be deeply involved in his or her life.

Coping with the Gray Areas

Part of parenting, especially when your children are becoming young adults, is learning to cope with the need to give answers when you don't know for sure what those answers should be. It requires a lot of thought, and while the relationship you've built with your kids will help them accept your decision, it doesn't make the decision for you. Dealing with that uncertainty is hard, but it's absolutely necessary if you're going to maintain your role as a protective and guiding parent as your child grows up.

When I became a mom, I was uncertain many, many times. Sometimes I felt inadequate, thinking I had missed out on some giant piece of knowledge that should have been imbued in me when my daughters were born. If there is, indeed, some deep archetypal wisdom that we parents should have naturally, I must have been absent the day they handed it out. Sometimes I was in doubt, even dumbfounded. Sometimes I just didn't know how to handle things. I suspect that, for every parent and stepparent, there are things that make you go, "Hmmm"—just like there were for my daughters and me.

Andrea made me think a lot. Responding to her unique way of asking me about things was easier when she was younger and most answers were either black or white, but when she became a teen, it was much more difficult. Most of her requests weren't in the realm of strictly good or bad but rather fell into the domain of appropriate or inappropriate. I often wondered if she really needed me at all. We had talked so much throughout the years that she knew how I thought, what I believed, how I set boundaries, and why. That's where we found our-selves the night she asked me if she could go to her first homecoming dance. I was visiting my sister, so she called me long-distance to ask my permission. She was only in the eighth grade, and the dance was a *high school* event.

Andrea was always a challenge for me simply because she was so darn logical. She considered every detail in advance, and prepared a rebuttal for my response. Typically, she'd present her request with all the reasons she'd trumped up to support it. Then, pausing only for a quick breath, she'd submit, with equal fortitude, the concerns she knew I'd have regarding her request. Hesitating only long enough for me to absorb and appreciate how carefully she'd thought the whole thing through, she'd plunge forward with her final argument, which, of course, solidified the justification of the original request. She was formidable—she could have been a lawyer!

It usually took me a few moments to compose myself and gather my thoughts after one of Andrea's presentations. This case was no exception. I asked questions more to gain time than to gather information. She had put a lot of time and effort into her request. To show respect for her as well as for her careful thinking, I talked with her. There really was no right or wrong in the matter, but for me it seemed inappropriate that she advance herself beyond her years to participate in an event intended for older kids. Although we used that word *inappropriate* a lot throughout the years, Andrea was still young. It broke her heart to hear a no based on nothing more solid than "that's inappropriate."

I admitted that time might prove my decision wrong, but at that moment I had to rely on my gut. It's important that parents realize we're not always right, but we're always the parents. It's a humbling responsibility to give the yeas and nays to another person's activities, knowing that those yeas and nays are formulating the very character of someone you love. It's even harder when you have to say no to something that your baby has his or her heart set on without a rock-solid reason. This situation was one of the few times Andrea got angry with me. I was sorry to have to disappoint her so terribly, and I understood that she was angry. But I still thought it would be better for her in the long term not to go, and so I had to stick to my guns.

During this early teen and adolescent time, Andrea was beginning to set and clarify her own internal limits. It was a particularly important time for me to be firm in my guidance. In her impressive book *Mother-Daughter Wisdom* (Bantam Dell, 2005), Dr. Christiane Northrup counsels that parents help their kids stand firm and develop their internal character when we maintain clear guidelines, enforce rules, and set limits. On page 298 she advises, "This is a time when a mother absolutely must assume her role as an authority who determines what is appropriate conduct for her daughter around thorny issues like dating, going out with friends, and the kind of experimentation with smoking, drugs, alcohol use, and sexuality that is now common in many middle schools."

I did assume my role of authority, and I was grateful that Andrea and I had a good, solid relationship to hold us up. The homecoming dance was one of those times when we agreed to disagree. I invited her to call me back if she wanted to talk about her anger. Sure enough, about a half hour later the phone rang again. Although she tried feebly to lobby me to change my mind, she knew it was a done deal. Mostly she expressed her disappointment and anger. Mostly I listened, told her I understood, and said I was sorry. Although nothing changed, she felt better being able to talk to me and express her feelings fully and safely.

I remember this incident clearly, but not because it was so unique or dramatic. It was another of those myriad situations where we parents merely slog our way through, and this one actually ended well, at least for our relationship. I've told Andrea that I hope I'm around when she has interchanges with her own teenager. If she looks around, she'll probably spot me off in the corner, smiling as I watch her struggle and try to find a way through the haze with her own daughter. We moms really do enjoy a little revenge now and then!

When You Think You've Made a Mistake

When I was a child, my dad spanked me one time. Although I have long since forgotten what I did to deserve this unusual punishment, I can still see my little body draped over the seat of a dining room chair, which was covered in a needlepoint cushion of chocolate brown with yellow flowers. One pop from the hand of my dad and it was over. The anticipation was much more powerful than the actual event. I also remember seeing the tears in my dad's eyes, afterwards, as he gave me a hug. Now I wonder if he was conflicted, confused, or sorry he'd done it.

Once when Carol was about thirteen, she screamed at me and spent much of the evening being over-the-top disrespectful to me. Not knowing quite what to do, I asked her to go to her room and grounded her for the weekend. By the second night I realized we weren't accomplishing anything. I decided I'd made a mistake in grounding her because I wasn't teaching her respect by shutting her up in her room. So I went to her and asked about what I had done to ignite her anger. Turns out she had been mistreated in school and took it out on me. As we talked, she apologized for being disrespectful, and I apologized for my hasty punishment. We both felt better so we cele-brated by going to the movies together. When we parents can't figure out how to handle a situation on the spur of the moment, we sometimes make the wrong decision. When I made mistakes, I tried to apologize quickly and begin again. Rather than making me seem weak and ineffectual, I think it made me seem more human and approachable. It also enhanced the trusting relationship between my daughters and me. If we don't hasten to make it right, we can cause a gradual fracture in the relationship, making discipline even harder in the future.

This is what happened to fifteen-year-old Julia the afternoon she got into a fight with her mom. She grumbled to me in my therapy office that she had asked her mom to drive her to town late one afternoon to hang out with some friends, but her mom was too busy and an argument ensued. Disappointed and angry, Julia bolted out of the house and

WHEN I MADE MISTAKES, I TRIED TO APOLOGIZE QUICKLY AND BEGIN AGAIN. RATHER THAN MAKING ME SEEM WEAK AND INEFFECTUAL, I THINK IT MADE ME SEEM MORE HUMAN AND APPROACHABLE.

was gone like a streak. Her dad couldn't find his cell phone, so he assumed Julia had taken it. Together, Mom and Dad concluded that Julia was hitchhiking to town because it was too far to walk and that she had stolen her dad's phone to contact her friends on the way. Since hitchhiking was strictly forbidden, they were distraught and worried and jumped in their car to try to find Julia along the highway, but to no avail. They returned home to get ready for their seven o'clock dinner reservation. When they left again, they decided to lock Julia out of the house to punish her for her disobedience.

In the meantime, Julia was merely walking in the woods, on a hiking trail near their home, trying to cool off her anger. She had not taken her dad's cell phone (he later found it in his jacket pocket), she had not hitchhiked to town, and she had not talked or met with her friends. When she returned home just before dark to a locked house, she found an open window and climbed inside. A couple of hours later, when her parents came back from dinner, she was watching TV in the living room, feeling sullen, unjustly treated, and betrayed. Her parents didn't know how to resolve the situation, so they didn't say anything, acting as though nothing had happened. It was only later, after subsequent arguments, that they decided Julia should go to therapy.

As Julia recounted her side of the story in my office, she shared with me what she had been thinking and feeling as she crawled into her house through the window. "I can't believe they locked me out of the house!" she cried, still incredulous. She thought they were cruel and abusive, and they had no heart. She wanted to lock *them* out of the house! She was furious and vowed to find a way to pay them back for how they were treating her and make them wish they had never done it. But most of all, she was hurt—down deep to the bone. She couldn't fathom that they wouldn't have known how it felt to be locked out of her own house like a criminal. Now she believed they didn't trust her at all and didn't know why they couldn't have waited to find out where she was before they jumped to conclusions. She agonized that they must not have known her at all or even cared about her. She said, "I thought we had something pretty good going between us, but if one dumb argument causes all this, then I guess not. I feel like I'm alone in the world with no one I can count on."

That one evening caused a serious breach of faith between Julia and her parents. Not because they jumped to conclusions. (Of course, parents shouldn't do that, but we're human and we're not perfect.) Not because they didn't know what to do and ended up doing the wrong thing—that'll happen too. But because they weren't quick to apologize and repair the damage. That's what can destroy the relationship for the long haul.

I've never known a parent who wasn't perplexed and befuddled at times, nor one who wasn't stymied and didn't know what to do. I've never known a parent who hasn't made mistakes—we all do. Sometimes we just mess up. Our kids are moving targets, and it only makes sense that we won't hit the mark every time. Like my dad, occasionally we'll find ourselves conflicted, confused, and sorry about how we reacted. Remember, we only have to be good enough, and that means be quick to acknowledge where we go wrong and be willing to start again.

Staying on the Same Team

Curfew. Even the sound of the word has a kind of dictatorial, punitive ring to it, yet every family has to deal with it in some form or another. When Carol and Andrea were in high school and most of the parents around us were setting curfews for their teenagers, I hesitated. I just couldn't get my arms around the idea that it would be either fair or logical to arbitrarily pick a time and then require that they be home on the dot of that hour, no matter what.

While I was hesitating, trying to figure out how to handle the issue, we stumbled upon a strategy that worked really well for us. Together, we agreed upon two general times they should be home—one time for weekdays and a later time for weekends—and then adjusted them if necessary to fit the individual situation. If the girls called me during the evening with a request to stay out later, and that request was reasonable, I gave my permission. If not, they came home at the appointed time.

For example, if there was a legitimate birthday party at a friend's house, the cake was coming out at ten-thirty, and their curfew was eleven o'clock, then they would have had to gulp down the cake and leave early, feeling like little nerds, just to be home by eleven. Instead, they could call me and say, "Mom, the cake is coming out at ten-thirty. Would it be okay if you picked me up at eleven-thirty instead of eleven?" Sure. It fits the occasion.

On the other hand, if the party was legitimately over at ten o'clock, and by ten-thirty couples were beginning to slither into quiet bedrooms and the drugs were beginning to be passed around in the corners, I did not want to have set up the idea that the curfew was at eleven. I'd rather have discussed the concept that when the party was over, I trusted them to make that decision and call me to pick them up, no matter what time it was. A curfew at eleven o'clock would stamp into their minds, as well as the minds of their friends, that they would be there until eleven no matter what. It wouldn't give them a chance to set their own standards and practice their own decision-making skills.

Then there were the situations that didn't exactly fit the plan. One was when Andrea was older, maybe seventeen. The phone rang about midnight and, of course, I'd been asleep. Waking a mom out of a dead sleep is not the best time to get clear thinking out of her, but Andrea already knew that when she dialed the number. As I recall, the conversation went something like this:

"Mom, we're over at Ryan's house and I'd like to spend the night."

"I've been asleep for a while. You'd like to what?"

"Spend the night. We've been playing pool on Ryan's dad's pool table and everyone got tired. Most of the kids are already crashed. It's just that we're really tired, and I'd come home early in the morning. I know you're worried about alcohol, but nobody's drinking. We've just been playing pool. It's totally fine and innocent. I'd like to stay. It really doesn't matter if I sleep here and come home early tomorrow or come home now and sleep. The only thing I'm going to do is sleep, and it's less dangerous to sleep when I'm so tired than to drive when I'm so tired."

"Andrea, you're talking too fast for me. I'm still asleep, and this doesn't sound like something I want to agree to. Who's there?"

"Ryan, three of his friends, and Brian and me."

"So, you're telling me that you, your boyfriend, and four other guys want to sleep over together in Ryan's house? And you want me to give my permission for you to do that?"

"Well, it's not like five guys and me. It just happens that there are no other girls here, but it's not about guys and girls, it's about being sleepy. The other guys are already asleep, Mom. It just seems safer to stay here and sleep now rather than try to drive home when we're so tired."

"You know, Andrea, you always have worked out the reasons why you want to do something before you even talk to me, but this one is over the limit for me. In addition, it isn't fair for you to wake me up at midnight and ask me to be wise and make a decision when my mind is still half asleep. If you had brought this idea to me earlier in the evening, when I could think better, we might have at least discussed it more, but considering that you waited this late, I'm going to say no.

"The lesson here is that you can't expect me to listen carefully to your reasoning when you bring it to me in the middle of the night. You may be upset and think I'm being unfair, but that's okay. I'm sorry, but please come home right away. And I always appreciate that you call me, even when you wake me up."

Andrea was home in minutes, not even angry with me. I always liked hearing her reasoning, and I always listened carefully to it—even when it included cockamamie ideas like sleeping over with five guys. In her defense, I suppose it was a pretty normal idea for someone her age, so I guess it didn't hurt for her to ask.

In contrast, there's Gracie, who came to my office some time back to talk about her thirteen-year-old daughter, Katie. It was a fairly typical scenario. Katie was beginning to feel her independence and wanted to assert it in any way she could. Although she may have felt unsure, even scared, on the inside, she was acting pretty cocky on the outside and was treating her parents as though they were dumb and old-fashioned. Katie wanted to stay out later than her parents wanted her to. They thought ten o'clock was late enough on a school night for a thirteen-year-old, but Katie wanted her curfew to be eleven. She was beginning to sneak out and lie about where she'd been. They were beginning to respond by locking down, setting the limits more rigidly, establishing rules, and creating parameters for grounding. All because they loved her.

Gracie and her husband wanted to do the right thing for Katie, but they didn't know what that was. They thought they had to get tougher and stricter, so instead of sitting down with Katie and opening lines of communication, they clammed up and got heavy handed. Instead of initiating dialogue, they initiated silence, which began to erode the relationship. Katie responded as you'd expect. She quit talking to her parents and became sneaky, obstinate, and grouchy. I cautioned Gracie to change her approach to her daughter because she was putting a wedge between herself and her husband and Katie, rather than creating an environment where they could work together. I feared that those wedges would only get bigger. I encouraged Gracie to talk with her daughter so that, as the stakes got higher, she would be *in* the loop, not strangled *by* the loop Katie had created with her peers.

We talked about how Gracie could sit down with Katie and start again from scratch to rebuild the relationship and the communication she had destroyed. This is what "scratch" might look like:

"Katie, I'd love to spend a little time talking together. I'm aware that we haven't done much of that recently, but I've learned some new things—about me, about you, and about us as mother and daughter. I'd like to implement some of them, and talking with you is one of them. I think I've glossed over some of the good parenting ideas we could have been using together, and I'm so sorry I haven't been as attentive to you and your issues as I wish I had been. I haven't been listening to you very well, but I really think it's never too late to start, and I want to start now."

Gracie could then acknowledge that she had laid down too many restrictions without being sensitive to Katie's feelings. Gracie could apologize for thinking about her own life more than Katie's. She could emphasize how sad she had become, realizing that they were no longer on the same team and that they didn't relate the way they used to. Gracie might then suggest that they start doing something together to reconnect and ask Katie if she'd like to join her for lunch, a bike ride, or a shopping spree. Katie might not jump at the idea, but if Gracie is willing to take her time and go slowly, they might be able to get their relationship back on track.

My approach to getting my daughters home safely at a reasonable hour would not have worked if we hadn't already had a good relationship. We would have been in for a lot of arguments, anger, sullen behaviors, and maybe even rebellion.

Trying to force your kids to comply with your demands just does not work very well. Of course, they have to be old enough and mature enough to understand the concept and think for themselves. Beyond that, it's about being open and honest with each other and making sensible decisions appropriate to each individual situation. Staying connected can actually make a potentially rough time a relatively easy one.

Dear Carol,

   Sometimes I think you wish you didn't have so many feelings—or at least that you didn't feel them so much. Over the years, I've learned that EVERYONE has feelings. It's just that some people stuff them down inside and don't let them out. That's not healthy.

   You're fortunate because you're not afraid of feelings— not yours or other people's, and that gives you a much greater opportunity to have intimate and really fulfilling relationships in your life.

   I love you bushels and nightgowns,

Mom

CHAPTER 4

More Common than Cowboy Boots at a Rodeo:

Dealing with Feelings in Your Family

WHEN MY EX-HUSBAND AND I were at the treatment center for his addiction, I was in pain. I felt confused and apprehensive about our future, but I listened with great interest to the educational presentations they offered there. The professionals knew something that the addicts did not know: *Holding in your feelings—not allowing yourself to get in touch with them or express them—can be hazardous to your health.* Allowing the wide range of feelings to bubble up into conscious awareness and then dealing with them appropriately presents one of the most difficult things for anyone to do. It's a vital part of recovery for addicts, it's essential for the well-being of any adult, and it's equally important for children. Our job as parents is to help our kids learn to acknowledge and express their feelings because that ability will help them to have healthier relationships throughout their lives.

Whether you are an adult or a child, if you're not accustomed to feeling your feelings, just experiencing the normal, day-to-day load can feel like an intense, life-threatening overload. It's often frightening to become acquainted with the feelings that live within your own body. Since some people have lived most of their lives shoving down, turning their backs on, and ignoring their emotions, those emotions have long since become strangers, even enemies. Often, thinking about embracing and becoming friends with your feelings can be a terrifying process.

Yet, a healthy lifestyle requires relationships, and healthy relationships—with special loved ones, with family, and with friends—require opening up and sharing the feelings inside. Your feelings make you huggable, touchable, lovable. Cutting off your feelings cuts you off from other people, isolating you and keeping you lonely. When parents model appropriate sharing of their feelings, they teach their children to do the same, and they provide a greater opportunity for kids to become happy and successful adults.

> **CUTTING OFF YOUR FEELINGS CUTS YOU OFF FROM OTHER PEOPLE, ISOLATING YOU AND KEEPING YOU LONELY.**

Some years back a young man came to see me for therapy because he knew something was wrong with his life. He slumped into the chair in my office just looking at me, expecting me to "fix him." I began gently and slowly because it was instantly clear to me that he was incapable of getting in touch with his feelings. He couldn't tell me whether he was sad or happy, disappointed or lonely, depressed or angry. He knew he didn't like how he felt, but he couldn't identify a single emotion. Not only had he grown up in a family that neither acknowledged nor talked about feelings, but he was most uncomfortable with his own, having ignored them all his life. The only descriptive word he could find to talk about himself was "upset." As we gradually explored various aspects of his life, he revealed that he was upset about his family—particularly his brother, who stole all his parents' attention—his job and his girlfriend. He didn't have many friends, but that was okay with him because, if he had more, they would probably just upset him anyway. He was trying to cooperate with me. He simply did not have the vocabulary or the experience of talking about what was going on inside him.

He couldn't initiate conversations about himself—what he wanted or what made him happy—and the answer to most of my questions was "I don't know." It took many weeks of therapy to help this young man identify that he was lonely, sad, and depressed, and many more to help him understand that so long as he was closed up and shut down, he wouldn't be able to have close relationships either—at least not the kind that would alleviate his loneliness, his sadness, and his depression. He'd be missing out because feelings make up a huge part of who we are.

As parents, our job is to make sure that our children never end up in the position of that young man. Often, a large part of ensuring that is making sure *we* are comfortable with feelings—both our own and those of our children.

Whoa, Feelings

Did you ever think about how many different emotions you—or your child—feel in one day's time? No doubt there are dozens, some of which you don't even have a name for. It's great when they boost you up, but sometimes they knock you down. They cause you to smile, frown, or freeze up, to burst into song or burst into tears. They guide your behaviors, direct your interactions with people, and dictate how you go through your day. And they do the same for your child. Because even young children feel a full range of feelings, parents need to be observant for clues as to how to help them deal with their feelings most effectively. If parents are uncomfortable with their own emotions, they naturally don't feel at ease with their kids' feelings either. Kids sense this and won't open up to anyone who can't handle what they have to say. This is one important reason why parents need to work out their own feelings—on their own—so they can be available for their children.

> IF PARENTS ARE UNCOMFORTABLE WITH THEIR OWN EMOTIONS, THEY NATURALLY DON'T FEEL AT EASE WITH THEIR KIDS' FEELINGS EITHER.

In the end, the best way for you to deal with your kids' feelings is to talk about them. Even when it's uncomfortable. Even when it's scary. Because if they don't express them, it can damage their emotional systems like a clogged sink with no drain.

Some feelings are more powerful than others. There are five feelings that most kids feel at some point in their growing-up years—feelings that are usually considered negative and can have a long-term effect. These five feelings are

- Depression
- Anger
- Guilt
- Fear
- Grief

When it comes to these feelings, parents play an important role in helping kids get their feelings out rather than holding them inside.

Feeling #1: Depression

Depression is a big feeling that can permeate your entire life. It can be caused by an event in the real world, or it can be a deeply rooted, on-going feeling that has no apparent basis in a person's day-to-day life. It can be such an isolator that it often breeds more depression. Being alone is okay, but feeling alone creates a sense of hopelessness and helplessness that can lead to grave mental illness and even suicide. The classic definition of depression is anger turned inward. When you don't get your anger out, there's no place for it to go, so over time it settles in like a thick fog. The anger you didn't express to anyone else you now take out on yourself, except that it takes on the dull, muted form of depression.

Have you ever noticed that small children are usually either bubbly and happy or crying and sad? They haven't learned to hide their feelings yet, so the whole world knows how it's going for them. As your children grow older, they learn to hold things in. They may be quiet or sullen or appear to others to be distant. You may find your child or teen to be lethargic and listless. They may have no appetite, no energy for friends or activities. They may be tired all the time, wanting to spend excessive amounts of time in bed. They may be uncharacteristically irritable and snap at people for little or no reason. Jokes aren't funny; life is no fun. They act as if they have nothing much to look forward to.

Once when I described these characteristics of depression in my parenting course, one parent raised her hand and remarked, "That sounds like the normal description of a kid going through adolescence." Everyone in the class laughed and nodded agreement. It's true: There are times when depression and adolescence *do* resemble each other. During the adolescent and teen years, kids are especially sensitive to such events as being ridiculed by peers, humiliated by a teacher, and dismissed by a circle of friends. They get emotionally knocked down if they're not picked for a sports team, not invited to a school dance, or snubbed by friends. Whether it's major depression or momentary depression, you need to have regular, daily contact with your children so you understand what's happening in their lives. It's not easy for kids to share their emotions because it makes them feel vulnerable and exposed, so the default is choosing to keep them bottled up. You need to let them know you care by being patient, taking time to just be with them, and *not* interrogating them or forcing the issue. You can help your children a great deal simply by being available and lending a nonjudgmental, kind, and listening ear. However, sometimes these steps aren't enough. We can't always help our kids out of the hole they're in, so if you're not sure what to do, don't hesitate to call a professional for help.

Feeling #2: Anger

Once when I was driving down Main Street on a quiet morning, I slowed down at the intersection because a city bus was blocking my view of pedestrians at the crosswalk. As I crept into the intersection, sure enough, a pedestrian not yet in my view was waiting for me to pass by. Normally, I would have stopped to let her walk through, but since I was already in the intersection, and she was already stopped, I drove on. A minute later, I pulled into the gas station to fill up and was greeted by an irate stranger who stuck his face into my car window and angrily railed me about how careless I was and how he should report me to the police for reckless driving and for almost killing a pedestrian. Stunned at his outrage, I simply stared at him in disbelief. There have certainly been times when I've made a foolish maneuver while driving, but this wasn't one of them.

This guy was hoppin' mad, but I'll bet he had something stuck in his craw before he spotted me. I may have pulled the trigger for his anger, but something else had loaded the gun. Maybe he'd had a fight with his wife that morning. Maybe he'd just come from his office where he'd found out that a colleague had betrayed him. Unfortunately, you don't get rid of your anger by firing it at the wrong person. After the explosion, it just sinks back in, ready to come shooting out again and again until you finally figure out who it belongs to and address it with the right person.

If a parent hasn't addressed his or her own anger and dealt with it in an appropriate way, you can be pretty sure it will spill out at home, causing confusion and fear in the kids. They'll learn the lesson that their parent is irrational and inconsistent and won't be likely to share their own feelings.

A lot of times people don't even know they're holding anger inside, and they're as surprised as anyone when a two-ton rocket comes blasting out from a two-pound incident. Other times, people have been overreacting for so many years that they don't even know their reactions are overboard. They live with a tangled pile of wrath inside, like a nest of snakes, ready to strike at any moment. They think it's normal to give you the finger if you accidentally turn in front of them at the

> IF A PARENT HASN'T ADDRESSED HIS OR HER OWN ANGER AND DEALT WITH IT IN AN APPROPRIATE WAY, YOU CAN BE PRETTY SURE IT WILL SPILL OUT AT HOME, CAUSING CONFUSION AND FEAR IN THE KIDS.

intersection. They think it's ordinary to rage if their spouse forgets to bring home the Häagen-Dazs they asked for. They believe it's okay to get indignant at the ticket counter agent who announces that the flight has been delayed due to bad weather. And they often consider it totally inconsequential when they explode at their kids.

No one is wrong to feel anger. In fact, when something unjust happens to an emotionally healthy person, it's appropriate to feel those feelings. The Bible counsels us to be slow to anger. It doesn't say we should never get angry. There must have been an ancient understanding that anger is a normal feeling, well within the spectrum of human emotions. Although it's not bad to become irate, what causes us problems is when we can't forgive, we can't let go, and we simmer and seethe over time. Anger can then develop into resentment, bitterness, and the desire for revenge—crustier feelings that attach themselves more tenaciously.

When Carol and Andrea got mad at me, I invited them to blurt out their feelings to me. The rule was that they could be intense, even loud, and they could list every feeling they had. They just had to express it appropriately, meaning no bad language, no disrespectful comments, and no below-the-belt accusations. The anger belonged to them, so they were encouraged to keep their pronouns in the first person, not switching to *you, you, you*. They could expound on their feelings as long as they wanted to, and if once wasn't enough, they could come back at it again. I wanted them to know that I would listen and consider their commentary. The goal was to get it out of their system so they wouldn't have a snarled mess of it to carry around, weighing them down as they went through life.

Feeling #3: Guilt

Guilt isn't just universal, it comes in an array of flavors. When Andrea was in the fifth grade, she and a couple of friends cooked up a mischievous plan at school one day. During lunch they organized a snowball fight behind one of the buildings at school. They were clever enough to devise their little prank, but evidently not clever enough to keep from getting caught. Guilty on the spot! They were punished: First, they had to sweep out the school buses, then they were to clean the lunch room for the next week. This kind of guilt is easy to deal with. Being pronounced guilty simply confirms the truth. If you're guilty of misconduct, the punishment clears your conscience.

The other kind of guilt is more troublesome. A lot of us feel guilty for things we never were and never did, and it makes us feel bad about ourselves. Our guilt is deeply rooted inside our brains from messages ingrained in us by the world around us—families, churches, and significant others in our lives. Guilt doesn't make us more effective or more productive. It only damages our self-esteem. To keep that from happening to our kids, it's our responsibility to be careful how we talk to them.

Here's what not to say: "I can't believe you stayed out late on a snowy, icy night without calling to let me know you were safe. I was worried sick." That's an accusation and makes your child feel guilty for being bad and wrong.

Instead, try this: "Oh, Susie. I'm so glad you're home safely. I was worried when you didn't call. Next time, please let me know that you're okay." This teaches without making Susie feel guilty.

Having grown up in a "hellfire and damnation" church, where I was made to be afraid and feel guilty about so many things I did, I knew I had a lot of guilt in my background. As an adult, I worked hard to get rid of that feeling that seemed to drape over me like a wet blanket. However, since I had become accustomed to the feeling early on, I thought it seemed likely that I could easily lay it onto Carol and Andrea, albeit unwittingly. I asked them to let me know every time I said or did something that made them feel guilty so that I'd have the chance to rectify it immediately. Carol took me up on the offer instantly. I was horrified to realize how many subtle comments I made that produced guilt. I was equally amazed that she could actually feel the guilt so quickly after I had made the remark. Kids soak up everything we parents dole out to them; I'm grateful that we had a relationship that made them feel safe to let me know when I dumped my old baggage on them. It gave me a chance to apologize and work on correcting my behaviors.

Often we say things to our kids that make them feel guilty. But whether we're the ones who make our children feel guilty or whether their guilt comes from another source, talking about it is the best way I know to help them understand it and work through it.

Feeling #4: Fear

One emotion everyone knows kids feel is fear. Often young kids get scared because the world is still unfamiliar to them and everything is a new experience. When Carol was a toddler, a huge dog trotted up to her with his giant tail wagging and his big, wet tongue hanging out. I'm sure she thought he was going to eat her alive. No wonder she ran to me in terror, crying out how scared she was. I could have said, "Don't be afraid. He's not going to hurt you," but that would have invalidated her gut feeling and begun to give her the message that she couldn't trust her own instincts. Instead, I held her, comforted her, affirmed that the dog was big, and validated her feeling of fear. Then slowly, we went together toward the dog and allowed him to lick her. This enlarged her experience and allowed her to change her own feeling, replacing fear with pleasure.

Having a strong bond with your kids gives you the opportunity to talk about their fears at every age. It can also give you a chance to help them learn that bravery is not the absence of fear but rather taking appropriate action in the face of fear. Whether it be encouraging them to ski down a difficult slope, speak in front of a large group of people, or confront someone about an inappropriate action, talking with your kids about their fears can help them to overcome obstacles to their success.

Feeling #5: Grief

Grief is one of the hardest feelings. I'll never forget the day Carol was hit with the loss of a classmate, perhaps her first boyfriend, in middle school. He had died instantly in a skiing accident, having fallen into a mine shaft hidden in the trees. It was a tragedy beyond anyone's imagination, the nightmare of every parent. The entire town was in shock and grief. I held Carol as we went over the details of the accident again and again, as we talked about life and death, as she asked questions for which I had no answers. She shared her dreams about him, and we talked about how, even in her sleep, she was trying to come to grips with her loss.

It takes more time than most people think to process grief. Just when everyone else thinks your grieving period should be done, you're in the deepest part of it, so don't try to rush your children to the other side. Sometimes all you can do is just be there to cry with them. Sometimes there are no words, but the warmth of your body next to theirs can give more comfort than you imagine. You never know how other people feel in the depth of their mourning, so don't pretend that you do. Often, telling them you *don't* know how they feel—how painful and sad it must be for them—makes you seem more reliable and gives them courage to share their grief. Talking helps immensely, so be careful not to censor anything they say as they're pouring out their pain.

In our family, we shared our grief when we lost our dogs, one by one, and of course when my ex-husband and I separated, when my father died, when Andrea's dear friend's dad was killed in a plane crash. These are terrible losses, but what about those smaller, more personal losses—like when Carol didn't get chosen for the volleyball team, or when the guy she liked didn't ask her out the second time, or when she got dissed by a friend, or when a hope evaporated into thin air, a dream burst open, or a plan shattered? These may seem like insignificant losses, but every single one creates a small mound of emotional ashes that accumulates into a heap over a lifetime, each new loss stacking up on top of the last. These are the times you want to be there for your kids, walking by their side. These are the important times for parents to be listening—and talking with their children.

Recognizing the Importance of Feelings

There are no good or bad feelings. Feelings just *are*. They're with us all the time, every single moment. We may not be aware of them, but we have emotional responses to everything we do and everything that happens to us. They may be subtle or they may be intense, but they are never absent, and feeling them is never wrong or bad. It's important to let children understand this, and to let them know that all of those feelings are okay to have and to talk about.

As a therapist, I have made feelings my bailiwick. In my practice, I've spent countless hours digging into and exploring the feelings of my clients, helping them to sort out dysfunction, repair damages, and start anew. I've felt their pain, connected with their despair, listened to their brokenness, and tried to create hope. This is what I have learned: If we don't acknowledge our feelings, they can make us become emotionally unavailable. They can cause disconnection and an inability to deal with others. People can detach from their own inner being, not knowing who they really are or what makes them tick, thus becoming strangers not only to others but also to themselves. Sometimes people even become psychologically and physically sick from not acknowledging their feelings—sick from stress, ulcers, headaches, heart attacks, cancers, even seizures; the list goes on and on.

> IT'S NOT THE FEELINGS THEMSELVES THAT HARM YOU. IT'S ONLY WHEN YOU'RE UNAWARE OF THEM— WHEN YOU DON'T ACKNOWLEDGE, EXPRESS, OR DEAL WITH THEM—THAT THEY CAUSE PROBLEMS.

It's not the feelings themselves that harm you. It's only when you're unaware of them—when you don't acknowledge, express, or deal with them—that they cause problems. When you don't acknowledge them, they can clog you like wet tar. Feelings are more common than cowboy boots at a rodeo, and acknowledging them is as important as acknowledging hunger or fatigue, the need for exercise, or the desire to be with another person.

Giving Feelings a Place in the Family

I wanted to make sure my kids weren't afraid of their feelings, so I tried to model for them how to talk about them. By sharing my emotional life with them, I demonstrated that it was okay for them to share theirs with me. For me, feelings are what make our lives full and juicy instead of dried up and boring. They bring us to life from the inside out and make us unique and interesting. I was always eager and pleased to hear my daughters express their feelings.

That's why I was saddened over the years by clients who had never learned to get their feelings out in the open. Too many came to therapy bogged down in leftover feelings from childhood and adolescence. They had tamped those feelings down for years, with never an opportunity to feel them, let alone express them aloud.

> FOR ME, FEELINGS ARE WHAT MAKE OUR LIVES FULL AND JUICY INSTEAD OF DRIED UP AND BORING.

Let me give you a snapshot of a few of these dear people who represent some of the stories I was told in my office. One man tried to describe what it was like for him to sit around the dinner table, afraid to say anything for fear his father would blow up in anger and clobber the entire family with it. Another told me how cold and impersonal it felt to be part of a family that only exchanged daily schedules and objective details; no one ever showed any emotions at all. Another related that his father got angry often, but no one else was ever allowed to be angry. Still another described a family that didn't hug or touch. Yet another explained that whenever she got bubbly and overly excited, she was told to calm down. Another related that she was repeatedly molested sexually by an older brother, but she knew she couldn't tell her mom or dad for fear of being disbelieved and harshly reprimanded. All of these people grew up uncomfortable with their feelings and unable to articulate them.

Families discourage the expression of emotions in a variety of ways. For some, it's okay to share the good things you do, but nobody wants to hear about the mistakes. In others, if you take courage to share the mistakes, you're ridiculed or punished. Other families convey the subtle message that they just can't handle you saying anything that would upset the smoothly rolling apple cart. They prefer to dance around the elephant in the kitchen, ignoring it totally, rather than to openly acknowledge the problem no one will admit to seeing. In many families, feelings are pretty scary. It's uncomfortable to feel them and unacceptable to talk about them, so kids grow up stuffing them inside, modeling themselves on their parents, who probably learned their own stuffing techniques from Grandma and Grandpa.

One of our parental obligations is to create a home environment in which all family members feel safe to express their feelings. A home is a safe haven only when feelings are welcome. It's a more genuine place to grow up, it's more fun, and it provides a better opportunity for your kids to have healthy relationships in their adult lives.

When I've talked with parents in my therapy office about expressing feelings with their kids, some give me a blank look. "I haven't been doing that," they say. "I'm not sure I even know how. Is it too late to start now?" I assure you it's never too late to start, no matter how old your kids are. We start new things in our lives all the time—new exercise patterns, new eating plans, new work routines—so why not new emotional habits? You can start today: Don't pretend. Don't minimize. Share it the way it is.

When you share your feelings with your kids, they see an example for how they can share theirs with you. This is what makes you accessible to your kids, keeps you connected with them, and makes you the one they want to talk to and listen to about the difficult stuff in their lives.

Helping Kids Express Intense Emotions

Carol and Andrea were only eight and ten when their dad and I separated. I'm sure they felt it coming for several months, as did I, but when he finally left, it threw us into a tailspin. I was devastated, thinking I would now be in the category of failed marriages. I was humiliated, because no one in my family had ever gotten a divorce. It had never been in my repertoire. My whole body, mind, and soul were surging with an odd mixture of love and hate that probably only someone who's gone through a bad divorce would understand.

I felt anger, fear, and confusion. I was so disappointed that things had turned out like this. My sadness was colossal and heavy. I felt intense loss in the present, and I grieved over our lost future because I saw my hopes and dreams swirling down the drain. I felt so lonely going through the most agonizing and heartbreaking experience of my life by myself. I felt betrayed and even violated. The fact that someone was actually leaving me shot down my confidence and made me feel fragile.

I was also worried about how the three of us would move on. One of the biggest pressures bearing down on my heart was my feeling of guilt over how our divorce would affect my children. I was completely devastated by the thought that our actions would hurt them in any way, and the mere notion that I was now a part of something that I was afraid would scar them was intensely painful. Depression bobbed in and out. I remember saying to their dad, "You've shattered me, but you don't have the power to destroy me." The determination that I would not allow anyone to destroy me kept me alive in those first several weeks and months.

As you can imagine, my emotions whirled inside me like a cyclone. Because I felt a literal pain in my chest, I visited my physician and asked her to check out every possible source of a heart attack. She tested me thoroughly and assured me my heart was in tip-top shape and the pain was emotional, so I went to therapy and tried to explain to the therapist that my emotions were so fierce that I was afraid I was going to die. She reassured me that I wasn't going to die, that I was simply vibrantly alive with feelings. Vibrantly alive with feelings?! That was certainly another way to frame it, and I tried to hang onto that idea like a drowning person to a buoy. It helped, and I've since used that very image with numerous clients who were struggling with intense feelings.

I describe this period of my life in detail so you can see how absurd it would have been to try to hide my feelings from Carol and Andrea and pretend everything was okay. While I was riding my own emotional bucking bronco, my daughters' lives had also been turned upside down. When their dad packed up and moved out, all three of us were left feeling as if there'd been a sudden death in the family. He was there, and then in an instant he was gone.

Obviously, I'm not an authority on my daughters' feelings. Each person is always the only expert of his or her emotional system. But I do remember some of what we went through together, and I feel confident in saying that both of them were also "vibrantly alive" with feelings.

The details of my divorce are most likely unique to me, but the feelings we all felt and the emotional havoc it caused for my kids and me are quite common. Most people going through this kind of family trauma experience a similar range and intensity of feelings, because under the surface we're all pretty much the same. Even though it may have seemed that way to us at the time, none of our feelings was unique. How we dealt with them, though, was somewhat unusual. Families who choose to put their feelings in the forefront, taking the time and effort to acknowledge and express them, aren't the norm. Our culture doesn't really support this kind of openness. Yet it's not rocket science—you don't need an advanced degree or any special training to do what needs to be done in these difficult situations, which is to deal with the feelings just as much as the events that trigger them.

The first thing we did together was cuddle, hug each other, and cry. It was a great release because I think it helped us get our feelings out before we had any words to describe those feelings. We also hugged a lot because I wanted to comfort them body to body, to let them know through the pores in their skin that I loved them and would never leave or abandon them.

SOMEBODY ONCE SAID THAT NAMING YOUR FEELINGS IS THE FIRST STEP TOWARD TAMING THEM.

Next we talked. They asked a lot of questions. I could answer some of them, but others just hung in the air, open-ended, posing only more questions. Why did he do it? What will happen to us, and will we ever be a happy family again? I never lied to them, circumvented their questions, or changed the subject. I always tried to assure them that, no matter what, we'd be okay.

Somebody once said that naming your feelings is the first step toward taming them. In the early weeks, my girls' feelings were wild, and as I encouraged them to let their feelings tumble out, I realized just how tempestuous they were. The words they used expressed shock, horror, fear, confusion. They were also humiliated to go back to school and have to tell their friends that their parents were getting a divorce. It felt as if this would ruin their lives forever. To help calm them and let them know they weren't the only kids in school who had gone through this, we actually went through the school directory and noted how many students had a mom and dad with different addresses.

They were so angry at their dad for leaving that they said they hated him. Rather than telling them not to be angry or that they should not hate anyone, I made it safe for them to say it as many times as they wanted. They had a right to be angry. They felt that their foundation had just been crumbled by an adult they had trusted. I knew that the best way for them to process their anger and get it out was to express it. This was an important time to impress upon them that there are no bad feelings, and that they were never bad to feel them. Shouting out the anger at home didn't hurt anyone and was a healthy way for them to expel it from their bodies. I also knew that they really loved their dad, and their feelings of hate were a temporary result of disappointment. When talk failed, they could just scream or groan. Carol, holding her emotions close to the surface, used to get her feelings out by pounding the bed with pillows or ripping the newspapers into shreds. Andrea has always been a little more internal and contained with her feelings. Because she felt safest writing her feelings, I bought her a notebook to use as a journal and for writing letters addressed to her dad, which we never sent to him. It was her chance to express every feeling she had without even thinking about any negative ramifications.

Like a detective, I watched for signs of their feelings rippling to the surface; then I tried to offer a sanctuary for them, creating a safe place for them to talk whenever they wanted to. My goal was to be able to understand their feelings so well that they could really feel my sympathy and support. I wanted them to know they were strong and resilient, and although they hurt deeply, we would come out the other side healthy and happy.

Sharing feelings goes both ways in families with close relation-ships. Listening to them share theirs with me was healing not only for them but also for me. I think everyone benefits when the environment is receptive to authentic expressions of emotion with no judgment or critique. I wanted to be as open and transparent with them as they were with me, but without crossing the line into burdening them, worrying them, or making them my confidantes. Rather than giving them a message that I was untouchable, I wanted my life to touch them unreservedly, so I exposed myself to them undisguised to the extent I believed would be helpful to them. I shared feelings but tried to keep them focused on me, without overflowing into negative thoughts, feelings, or stories about their dad. If their questions prodded me to go over my boundary, I simply told them I thought it not right to talk to them about it. They knew I kept a journal. They knew I talked with friends because sometimes I closed the door and told them I'd be talking about things that would be inappropriate for them to overhear. They knew I saw a therapist. Sometimes parents hide the fact of their therapy from their kids as though it's a weakness and a humiliation, but I wanted them to know I was doing everything I knew how to get healthy and joyful again.

Even though I felt crummy, I tried to ski and be outdoors as much as possible, knowing that physical exercise is a great stress releaser. They knew I prayed, and often we prayed together. I'm sure my hugs helped them, but I'm not sure they ever knew how much their hugs helped me. In fact, I often wondered how difficult it must have been for their dad not to feel, as I did every day, their soft little bodies enveloped in my arms. In that, I was so blessed. I even cuddled with Nicky, our loving springer spaniel. He gave me uncanny instinctual and faithful sympathy when my emotions were running high. Even though Nicky otherwise never got up on the furniture, he couldn't give me enough comfort until he gradually, slowly, one paw at a time, crawled up onto my bed and snuggled himself flat against me.

We scraped through that experience, as most families do, whirling, swirling, and rolling sideways at times. I don't think my ex-husband fared quite as well in some respects. Years later, after we became friends again, he told me that he'd gone through some pretty significant health issues during that period. I'm convinced it was because he didn't have anyone to talk to or share his feelings with.

Over time, giving our feelings a prominent position in our lives, we began to change, grow, and heal. All three of us learned that, even though we get knocked down, we can rise up stronger than before. We began to laugh again and to share our joys as we had shared our pain. I'm convinced that our relationship made all the difference for us. We had begun sharing the feelings that formed the basis of our relationship many years before, so when the storm of divorce hit, the tools were already sharpened and ready to use.

Thank goodness, not every family experiences the ravages of divorce, but I can almost guarantee that there will be times in your life when your family will go through some trauma or other that will cause intense feelings. No one gets through life unscathed. Emotions can be crippling. The shock of sudden or extreme pain can numb people into personal isolation. If your family culture tamps down or hides feelings, it's much harder to reverse the pattern during a crisis.

> I CAN ALMOST GUARANTEE THAT THERE WILL BE TIMES IN YOUR LIFE WHEN YOUR FAMILY WILL GO THROUGH SOME TRAUMA OR OTHER THAT WILL CAUSE INTENSE FEELINGS.

Even if there are no huge crises, every family experiences ups and downs. Day-to-day difficulties can be sufficient to create harmful repositories of repressed feelings if they aren't regularly disclosed. It doesn't require anything nearly as dramatic as death, divorce, serious illness, or a tragic accident to erect giant piles of stored-up feelings that can haunt you as you try to move forward in life. In fact, feelings pop up as routinely as dandelions in springtime, so parents are wise to create an environment in which sharing them is automatic. Especially during the hard times, it pays off big when parents and their kids can stay connected and talk about feelings.

Love, Inside and Out

The love of parents for their children is like no other. All love grows when it's nurtured and dries up when it's not. That's because love is not only a noun—it's also a verb. It requires action. The feelings of love grow only as you continue to do loving actions. If you quit performing the acts, the feelings grow dim.

Throughout her lifetime my mom never quit doing loving actions for me, and they spilled out beyond me onto my daughters. One of the memories I treasure most is that of my mother meeting Carol for the first time. She was only one day old, and we were about to be discharged from the hospital to go home. My mother had just flown in, and my husband had picked her up at the airport and driven her directly to the hospital.

I was standing in the hospital corridor, holding Carol in my arms, when my mom rounded the corner and spotted us. The memory still brings tears to my eyes because it's a memory of unconditional love. The instant she laid eyes on us, still thirty feet away, her face softened into a beautiful warm smile; her eyes lit up with a radiant glow; she clasped her hands to her chest; and pure, unadulterated love exuded from her entire being. As she walked toward us, I felt the outpouring of her love for both of us. I marveled at the miracle of my mother's instantaneous love for a seven-pound, helpless stranger, but there it was.

My parents' love for both of my girls never faltered, and although we lived a thousand miles from them, they never decreased their loving actions toward Carol and Andrea and never forgot to do special things for them. The way my parents treated my kids was an extension of how they had always treated me—with respect, pleasure, and love. I believe their love for my daughters enhanced all of our lives.

Sadly, I think love can also flip, mutate, and become a life suppressor rather than a life enhancer. Instead of providing patience, understanding, support, and kindness for a child, a parent's love can veer off into some kind of self-centered behavior that ignores or endangers the child's well-being. In graduate school I became good friends with a guy whose family life wasn't as fortunate as ours. This is the story he told me.

Kevin grew up with an abusive mom and an absent dad. Having been raised by two alcoholic parents, Kevin's mom had never felt the actions of consistent and unconditional love. As a child she was often neglected and sometimes even abandoned for many hours at a time. As an adult she became so needy and insecure that all her behavior was directed to filling herself up with what she hadn't gotten as a child.

Then came her children. By the time the youngest, my friend Kevin, was born, his mom was so overwhelmed with chaos and responsibility that she made a sharp left turn away from loving actions and went into abusive behavior. She had apparently never learned to perform the actions of love because no one had ever done them for her. The feelings of love she must surely have felt for her children at one time became twisted and distorted into an ugly pathology.

Kevin sadly reported that he never felt loved by his mom. Instead, he spent an entire childhood fearing her and trying to avoid her impulsive and misdirected anger. Because he was the youngest, he was the easiest target. He received the brunt of her impatience, her craziness, and her wrath, but he didn't receive tenderness, understanding, or love. He was most certainly the recipient of her actions, but they were the actions of cruel words, manipulations, threats, and repeated physical abuses. They were not the actions of love. She didn't stand up for him, nor did she protect him. Her actions were ego driven, looking out for herself instead of her son.

Before he was eleven, Kevin's parents divorced, and because he was still a child, he stayed, along with his siblings, with his mom. He told me her actions then became even more desperate and more violent. She tried to force him to tell her that he loved her. Once, when they were walking down the street and he hovered fearfully behind her, she told him to walk alongside her or she would take him into the alley and hit him. Another time, she beat him in a clothing store dressing room until it drew the attention of the store clerks. Routinely, she slapped him again and again and struck him until he was sore and bruised.

One day Kevin's mom lashed out at him for something he hadn't done. In an instant of clarity, he stood up to her for the first time in his life. He was now fourteen and big for his age. This defining moment changed Kevin's life as he grabbed his mom's abusive arm and told her she would never again lay a hand on him. At last he realized he didn't have to be her victim any longer. Instead of seeing the error of her ways, she turned her back on him and kicked him out of the house permanently, after which he went to live with his father. It's hard to imagine what could possibly have gone so wrong with a mother's love that she could banish her fourteen-year-old child from home.

As far as I know, Kevin's mom has blundered through her life not ever having taken the courage to look inside herself and examine the things that went wrong. As for my friend Kevin, he's still learning to love himself and to trust others, because when you don't learn the consistent actions of love as a baby and a child, it's much more difficult to learn them later on.

Eden Ahbez wrote a song titled "Nature Boy" that was made popular by singer Nat King Cole. My favorite line in the song is, "The greatest thing you'll ever learn / Is just to love and be loved in return." Not everyone receives enough love to learn how to love themselves or others in a healthy way. If love is the greatest thing we'll ever learn, then it's the moral obligation of parents and stepparents to teach this beautiful feeling to our children by treating them with consistent and caring loving actions.

In therapy we sometimes say that feelings are our only reality. We may remember the facts wrong, but we always remember the feelings that went with those facts, whether they are distorted or not. That makes our feelings a very powerful part of who we are, what we think and how we interact with others. If we have strong, trusting relationships with our children, we will be able to help them understand the importance of their feelings, the value of learning how to express them, and the role those feelings play in creating successful lives.

Dear Andrea,

      I am so sorry for you and everyone who knew and loved your friend. It is tragic beyond words that she took her own life. I can't answer why she might have done it. There are so many complicated reasons. Over the years I've had clients who were on the brink of suicide, and usually it had to do with feeling like life was too overwhelming to handle, or feeling like they were in a tunnel with no light at the end and no way out.

      Often the only thing that prevented them from doing it was their feeling of being valued and loved and their deep understanding that they belonged to other people and that other people belonged to them. That makes a sense of belonging not only pretty basic, but an amazingly deep-rooted and a very important thing, doesn't it? I hope you always feel that you belong, that you are important to me, and that...

      I love you bushels and nightgowns,

          Mom

CHAPTER 5

The Buoy That Keeps Us Afloat:

Giving Your Kids a Sense of Belonging

CREATING A SENSE OF BELONGING in your family—a feeling that you are all important to each other, you're all part of the same team, and that you value each other—is one of the most important things you can do as a parent. If your kids *don't* feel like they belong, the consequences can become grave. I'm reminded of two clients who mirrored each other in their separate need to belong.

The first was Gary, about fifty years old when he came to see me. His dad was an army guy who thought it too sissy-like to hug his son or give him affirmations of any kind. Strict discipline was the rule by which they all lived, and bending the rules would have been more difficult than bending a steel rod. Gary's mom was softer but could hardly do anything other than follow her husband's commands. Poor little Gary received very little nurturing while he was growing up, and he was sent to military school the second he was old enough to be accepted. His parents wrote to him infrequently, and phone calls were even more infrequent. They seemed to be satisfied to receive notes from the school about his conduct and grades. During vacations, Gary sometimes went home with a friend. During shorter breaks, his parents were the only ones not to show up, leaving him at school, the only one in his dorm. Needless to say, he didn't feel that he belonged to anyone. He was convinced his parents didn't care about him.

As an adult Gary had been married and divorced twice. His first wife was unfaithful to him and his second left because she felt smothered by his neediness. Before and after his marriages, he'd had a series of unsuccessful relationships, including the one he was in when he came to therapy. In his current relationship, he bounced back and forth between draping himself around the woman he was with in a desperate need to feel attached to someone, and recoiling to the other extreme, distancing himself emotionally. Because he assumed she would leave him, as every other important person in his life had done, he didn't want to be too connected when it happened. It was his way of protecting himself from feeling the pain of abandonment again.

At first, Gary had no idea that his current relationship problems had anything at all to do with his parents. As we talked together, over time he began to be able to express the huge backlog of sadness about his childhood. Gradually, he realized that his need to belong, to feel loved, to feel important to someone was overwhelming. His healing began when he started dealing with his old pain with his parents and building, as an adult, the relationship he'd never had with them as a child.

A few years later, Monica came to see me. She had amazingly similar symptoms but came from a very different background. Monica had been forced into emotional isolation as a result of sexual abuse from her father and brother. She believed her mother heard the muffled noises in her bedroom and chose to collude with the insanity in their home. Monica's mom never intervened in any way, so Monica never felt she could trust her mother enough to talk with her. Since there was no communication in the family, Monica felt imprisoned in her agony. Like Gary, Monica felt as if she belonged to no one, that no one cared about her existence or her well-being. Also like Gary, her adulthood produced multiple marriages and chaotic relationships. She had no children, afraid that she would perpetuate the abuse of her own childhood, as well as the pain of always feeling alone and disconnected.

When Monica came to see me for therapy, she was in another relationship in which she, like Gary, vacillated between suffocating dependence and emotional shutdown. She threw herself on her boyfriend when the need to be a part of something overtook her, then cut herself off when the fear of being abandoned again became too great. For both Gary and Monica,

> OF ALL OUR YEARNINGS, OUR DEEPEST LONGING IS TO BELONG.

their lives were negatively affected because their parents had never given them basic care or made them feel like they belonged.

They both remind me of a therapy principle I learned from Virginia Satir, an important family therapy pioneer who had amazing insights into people and family dynamics. One of her theories that I like most goes like this: Of all our yearnings, our deepest longing is to belong. She likened us to an iceberg in that only the top 10 percent (our behavior) is visible from the surface. Everything else about us lies obscured below in the icy waters of our personality. At the very bottom, near the core of who we are, lie our deepest yearnings, the things we long for most. Satir believed these longings are universal because, inside, we're all pretty much the same. When we scrape away all our crusty defenses and get down to the heart, we all want to feel like we belong—to one special person, to a family, or to a loving group of friends.

Belonging comes packaged with a group of feelings and basic beliefs that help all of us move through our lives with greater ease, none of which Gary or Monica had. A sense of belonging leads to the feelings of being loved, cherished, and treasured. These feelings bring a sense of importance, worth, and value. The result is a realization: *I fit, I am a member, I matter, I am part of a team, they care about me.*

These are the gifts parents can give their children, quite different from what Gary and Monica received from their parents. Without these gifts, kids struggle even harder to keep their heads above water, floundering with their own self-esteem and having major difficulties in relationships.

Belonging is the buoy that keeps us afloat during difficult times. It's also the sail that bolsters the good life when times are happy. Without a sense of belonging, we're crippled, but *with* it we're much more capable of conquering anything life throws our way. I can think of no better way to achieve a sense of belonging than being an important, valued, respected member of a family.

Anointing Your Child

A few years ago my husband, Terry, and I attended a two-day workshop by Frank Pittman, a well-known psychiatrist, family therapist, and author. In that workshop, Dr. Pittman offered a different way of describing a child's need for belonging and acceptance. He told us that we need to *anoint* our children by regularly showing and telling them, both verbally and in actions, how great we think they are. Dr. Pittman's mandate was clear: Anointing children is such incredibly important work for adults that if we don't have kids of our own, we should even anoint other parents' kids.

Dr. Pittman pointed out that kids have a natural tendency to seek the approval of their parents. He emphasized how much our children yearn to be accepted by us and how they'll do almost anything to stand out, make an impression, or merely get a pat on the head from a parent. He also stressed how damaging it is to kids when they don't get anointed. Un-anointed kids have low self-esteem and act out with a whole range of unaccept-able behavior, including addictive, abusive, and violent behavior. Simul-taneously, they often spend the rest of their lives, even as adults, trying to measure up and please their parents. Being un-anointed negatively affects the decisions they make for their lives and their choices in mates as well as the quality of those relationships. In summary, the parental job of anointing is terribly vital.

> OUR CHILDREN YEARN TO BE ACCEPTED BY US AND THEY'LL DO ALMOST ANYTHING TO STAND OUT, MAKE AN IMPRESSION, OR MERELY GET A PAT ON THE HEAD FROM A PARENT.

Dr. Pittman's words of wisdom blew Terry away. He suddenly real-ized that as a kid, although he'd known that his dad loved him, he'd never felt anointed. His father had been too busy making a living for the family to watch Terry play football or compete in gymnastics meets. He hadn't taken the time to do anything to make Terry feel uniquely special or important. He never abused Terry or treated him poorly; he simply neglected to make him feel like a valued member of the family. He had not let Terry know that, as his son, he delighted his father's heart. As a result, Terry grew up feeling as though he wasn't quite good enough, and he never really belonged in his own family. Terry began to compete fiercely in gymnastics, becoming an All-American gymnast, hoping to finally gain approval and please his father. Then he left gymnastics, even though he had a chance to compete for a spot on the Olympic team, in order to delve into dental school, but nothing seemed to crack the flask and allow the anointing oil to flow from his father. Feeling as if it didn't matter what he did anyway, Terry left the family religion and strayed, searching for something he could fit in with. Fortunately for Terry, he was too busy studying to get into trouble, but he has lived most of his life with the emotional scars of believing he never pleased his father.

The saddest part for Terry, and the part that brings tears to his eyes every time he talks about it, is that he never learned the concept of anointing, so he didn't know how to do it for his own sons while they were growing up. Since he has learned the importance of belonging and acceptance, he has tried to start again and make up for the time he lost. It's a hard job to backtrack when your kids are already grown and gone from home, but that makes it no less worthwhile.

Soon after we attended Dr. Pittman's workshop, Terry presented his own version of Dr. Pittman's message to a large group of men who meet weekly for lunch to hear speakers and discuss issues of interest. Terry told me afterward that most of the fifty or sixty men at that lunch had a similar reaction to Dr. Pittman's message. The whole concept of anointing resonated within them. They instantly realized the validity of anointing their kids, but most of them also acknowledged their own deficits in taking the time and effort to actually do it. To this day, men who attended Terry's presentation occasionally meet him on the street and comment on the power and value of the lesson to anoint your kids.

Anointing your kids is a way to let them know how valuable they are to you and to the world. Here are two ways to anoint your kids:

- Affirm them
- Get involved

Anointing Tip #1: Affirm Them

Other cultures and other times in history seem to have understood this basic principle of affirming kids, but today we don't have many rituals or ceremonies to honor or anoint a child. There remain only a few. One established tradition is the cotillion, where young debutantes are officially introduced to the society with great pride. Latin cultures celebrate the *quinceañera*, where fifteen-year-old girls are ceremoniously presented to their families and friends. Bar and bat mitzvahs are another great example. It's no wonder Jewish kids study Hebrew so hard and take classes to learn about their religion, because at the celebration

> ANOINTING YOUR KIDS IS A WAY TO LET THEM KNOW HOW VALUABLE THEY ARE TO YOU AND TO THE WORLD.

they are anointed by family, friends, the rabbi, and the community, all of whom welcome these young people into their midst with the message that they do, indeed, measure up. It's a message that pronounces to all the world, "We think you have achieved, we're proud of you, you're good enough for us, and therefore, we're taking this time to celebrate *you!*" Wow! Very powerful and very affirming.

Affirming is important not only on one special day or at a single event; it needs to continue day by day. Be on the lookout for things your kids have done well. Notice when they exhibit a kind, caring, or helpful behavior. Watch for wise decisions and responsible actions and be eager to praise anything positive. But don't stop there. Inspire them and cheer them on to go the extra mile, persist when it's difficult, and try the really hard stuff. Your support means that you believe in them, and that's a huge affirmation.

It's not just about encouraging kids to do things that you think are appropriate, but rather celebrating them for being who they are and for doing what they enjoy and what they're good at. One child might choose to be a tennis player; another might become avidly interested in fishing. One could devote massive effort to becoming a cheerleader, the other to becoming a chess player or a member of the debate team. One might aspire to become an artist while the other is interested in flying or medicine. What's interesting about it all is that you as a parent might love all of these things or none of them. You might have a high regard for tennis but not for cheerleading. You might think that chess is a worthy cause because it sharpens the mind, but that fishing is a useless recreational pastime. The point is, it's not about you. It's about your children and what fits for them.

Anointing Tip #2: Get Involved

When you anoint your kids, you verbally encourage, praise, and support. You also have to bodily involve yourself in their activities—all the way from going to the park to push your two-year-old on the swing and playing catch in the backyard with your child whose idol is a famous baseball player, to canceling your own appointments to make those after-school soccer games. From watching the chess tournament and practicing hitting golf balls with your junior golfer, to standing in pools of water beside your child who throws flies to the trout. These are all ways to anoint your child, and they cannot be delegated. You must do them yourself.

I have a friend whose teenage son loved to fly-fish. My friend thought it was a useless and boring activity, so he never accompanied his son to the stream. Suddenly, he realized he was growing apart from his son and wanted to do something about it. He decided to try fishing as a way to reconnect. Since my friend knew nothing about fishing, he asked his son for tips, and soon they were chatting and having a great time together. My friend began to appreciate the talent his son had developed and his son began to feel valued by his father. Fishing brought them together and melted the distance between them. The principle behind getting involved is simple, but not easy to carry out even when there are two parents intentionally wired in to the issue. If you're a single parent, this may be even harder. We're all busy, and life gets in the way. There are many things that routinely separate us physically from our kids: work patterns, divorce, boarding school, kids' extra-curriculars. These make hands-on involvement in our kids' lives during the developmental years difficult, but it's still important. We have to be especially tuned in to the ways we can constantly create intimate connections that will make our kids feel special. If we don't, they'll surely go somewhere else to find that feeling, and we may not like the people or the groups to whom they turn.

> WE HAVE TO BE ESPECIALLY TUNED IN TO THE WAYS WE CAN CONSTANTLY CREATE INTIMATE CONNECTIONS THAT WILL MAKE OUR KIDS FEEL SPECIAL.

In his recent book, *Family First* (Free Press, 2004), Dr. Phil McGraw points out that the number one need in all people is the need for acceptance. Because kids want to feel like they belong, they cling fiercely to whatever group fills this need best. On page thirty-two he warns, "If that need is not met by your family, trust me, your kids will go elsewhere to seek it in order to find approval and acceptance." If we were anointed by our own parents, then we know how terrific it feels, and we need to make sure we're paying it forward to our own children. If we didn't get anointed when we were young, then we need to learn how to do it because it's worth it in spades to our kids.

"We're All in This Together"

Before I got divorced, I wasn't consciously aware of the ideas of anointing my kids or making them feel like they belonged. After their dad and I separated, I realized it was important for us to stick together, to feel like we were still a part of something—a solid unit like a home and a family. Thinking of ourselves as a team has been a helpful way of approaching it.

Perhaps by accident—not really by intention—my daughters and I hiked, skied, played, and traveled as a family. I believe it was the little things like conversations in the car and nature walks, not necessarily the mind bogglers like discussions about life and death, that made us feel that we belonged together. During the divorce, though, when much of our family life was swaying and teetering, it dawned on me that I'd better get very purposeful about bonding us together. We needed certain things we could count on, things that were stable, things we could put a stake into. In addition, the girls were getting older, and their natural inclination could be to drift away from our family to their

> **WE NEEDED CERTAIN THINGS WE COULD COUNT ON, THINGS THAT WERE STABLE, THINGS WE COULD PUT A STAKE INTO.**

friends unless I woke up to the need of making them feel how important, valued, and prized they were at home.

As we were shifting from a family of four to a family of three, it
was especially important to have rituals that didn't fluctuate. Carol,
Andrea, and I continued to have full home-cooked meals where we
three sat down together and reviewed our days. At the holidays we still
had our Christmas Eve hors d'oeuvres with sparkling apple cider while
we opened our stocking presents. Our celebration was as elegant as if we
were entertaining the queen, even though it may have been on
December 18, the night before the girls left to spend Christmas with
their dad.

From small to large decisions, I tried to approach the issues from
the perspective that my children and I were in this together. We discussed our weekend plans, where we wanted to go to dinner, whether we
would continue to go to church. We talked about when we were going
to clean out the garage, if it would work for me to go to a conference,
how I'd manage to get Carol to one event while simultaneously getting
Andrea to another. I remember emphasizing that we were still a family,
a solid family of three. I tried to keep us working together, cooperating
with each other, helping each other.

As life rolled on, I became very busy, but I tried to put my girls at
the top of my list. When I started working on my PhD, I cut out everything else that was possible to cut so I would still have time for them.
It was definitely a juggling act, writing research papers, keeping up a
private therapy practice, and being a single mom, but I wiggled my
schedule to make it to their soccer games and ski races. Probably every
single parent can relate to the stress of trying to squish far too much
into a tiny time slot. Balancing work and family has never been an easy
task, but we scramble to do our best. That's why I was astonished that

day when Andrea was in high school and we were looking at her photos of playing soccer in middle school—and she announced that she regretted that I'd never come to her games.

"What?!" I exclaimed. "Who do you think took these pictures? You have no idea how I moved clients and adjusted my work schedule to be able to watch you play. Of course, sometimes you and Carol played at the same time in different locations, so I had to race at halftime to the other field, sometimes in a nearby town, to make the second half for your sister. And you don't remember?"

I guess the lesson for parents is this: Don't even try to parent perfectly—just do the best you can and don't expect your kids to remember it all. There's support in a team, and it goes both ways. When I went back to school, I was overwhelmed, scared, and seriously lacking confidence. One evening during an orientation meeting, I called my kids. It was my nightly call, and I needed the two of them more than I wanted to admit. With each of them in turn, I shared my feelings of being intimidated and doubting my abilities. Carol said firmly and confidently, "Mom, I know you can do it; I totally believe in you." Andrea was equally affirming: "Mom, just think how great you're going to feel about yourself when you're finished."

> WHEN YOU TELL YOUR KIDS HOW IMPORTANT THEY ARE TO YOU, IT HELPS GIVE THEM A FEELING OF BELONGING.

At the time, and on many occasions since, I tried to express to my daughters how much I appreciated them and their encouragement, not only that night but also throughout my whole academic process. When you tell your kids how important they are to you, it helps give them a feeling of belonging.

Another example of our team came when I met Terry. Just ask him if he sensed our unity. He'd answer with an adamant yes. I'd been single for five years before I met him. I hadn't dated much—a guy with a gold tooth, a guy with bad breath. At least that's how the girls referred to them. What a subtle hint that they weren't ready for another dad. Then one day Carol announced that she was ready for me to meet someone. I wasn't actually aware that I'd been waiting for her approval, but who knows? Since we were deeply connected, maybe her subconscious was talking to mine, and I got the message that the timing hadn't been right until then. I don't really know what would have happened if my timing had disagreed with hers. I'm obviously not advocating that I should have lived my life according to her needs. I'm sure that if I'd been ready before she was, it would have been another of those many opportunities for us to talk it through. Let's face it. It's a pretty huge issue when a mom invites another man to live with her children and join the team.

Terry and I met only a couple of months after Carol's pronouncement that she was ready. He instantly scanned the scene and concluded that we came as a package. He knew without a doubt that we were a team. He'd get all of us or none of us, so he courted Carol and Andrea as sensitively as he courted me.

Carol was a pushover. All Terry had to do was give her big bear hugs and she was sucked in. Andrea was a little tougher to win over. She wasn't about to let just anyone take over as a father figure in her life, so Terry was watchful for when she needed Mom to herself and when it was okay to have an "intruder" in the family. When he could see that Andrea needed him to, he went home. Gradually, she realized that he would never—could never—disrupt the strong sense of belonging we'd already solidified. Given that nothing and no one would come between her and me, she was willing to make space in our family for another person. She'd already won his heart, and now she allowed him to win hers.

Carol, Andrea, and I were still a team of three because nothing could crack or fragment the bond of relationship and sense of belonging we'd created in the first fourteen and sixteen years of their lives. Now we were also becoming a team of four because they reeled in Terry— heart, line, and sinker.

Even at our wedding, I wanted Carol and Andrea to feel the strength of our own bond. Our wedding was about blending our two families. We stood in a meadow surrounded by a small circle of family and friends. The three of us stood with our arms around each other, facing Terry and his three sons with their arms around each other. I asked the girls, "There are more of them than there are of us, and they're bigger than we are. Should we do it?" As our wedding guests tittered and chuckled, my daughters' faces registered a moment of surprise before they stammered an affirming yes. I'd already known the answer to my question or I wouldn't have asked it, but what I was trying to say with my question to them was that we belong together, and nothing can ever splinter us apart.

Child Centered vs. Self-centered

Stephen's parents didn't understand the importance of giving their son a sense of belonging, so his story is a sad one. He came to see me for therapy when he was almost thirty years old. He'd stopped drinking and using drugs about a year before, been a regular attendee at Alcoholics Anonymous (AA) meetings, and now he was beginning to have the courage to explore his life at a deeper level in therapy.

Sensing that his current problems with relationships, his work, his decision-making process, and his friendships were all related to his history, Stephen began to tell me about his family and his childhood.

I report his story from his own perspective and with many of his own words.

Stephen was born into a wealthy family and received all the privileges money could afford. What he'd never gotten was a feeling of acceptance for who he was, nor a sense of his importance in his family. As he continued to relate stories of his growing up, he used phrases like "I never felt like I fit," "I was the failure in my family," "I was the one who caused all the problems," and "My parents couldn't wait to get rid of me."

Stephen was a mechanical genius, even as a small child. Taking things apart and putting them back together was his forte and his passion. Alas, his dad was always working and hardly had time to notice Stephen's special talent. His mom was busy with her volunteer organizations and her charity work and only complained about the messes he left behind from his projects. Nobody really cared. His skills and talents never meshed with what was valuable in the family, so he never felt he belonged there.

Stephen was a sweet but mischievous child, so conversations with him were usually directed at his problematic behavior. No pats on the head and no praise, just criticism. He was not a particularly good student, so communication often focused on his Cs and Ds. The tone was negative, the words sounded like lectures, the message was about his failure to match up. He didn't feel understood or valued for who he was. It seemed as if no one paid attention to him unless they were scolding him for doing something wrong, or threatening him to get him to behave differently. The words of praise he longed for went to his older brother, who caused no trouble and seemed to fit perfectly into the family scheme of things. Stephen was always on the outside.

Because of their money and power, Stephen's parents had a busy social life and were important members of their community. The feeling of being important washed over them, but none of it trickled down to Stephen. Instead, he felt like the odd man out. The nanny drove him to and from school and after-school sports. Dad didn't watch him play soccer or basketball because he was either in meetings or out of town on business. Sometimes Dad promised Stephen that he would be there, and Stephen allowed his heart to grow big with anticipation, but inevitably, at the last minute, something came up to prevent Dad from showing up. The same old message repeated itself in Stephen's young brain: "I don't matter. No one really cares about me. I'm not worth the trouble."

On the surface, the family seemed perfect. They looked good, but for Stephen everything felt hollow. In the empty void, he felt lonely, looked over, even cast aside. When he was younger, his parents sent him to posh summer camps, but he just wanted to be home where he might have a chance to interact with his dad. Later they shipped him off to Europe for summer school, but he longed to be with his family, where he might feel some nurturing from his parents. Instead of feeling like he belonged, he felt like they wanted him out of their lives.

Meanwhile, his parents continued their good life, never bending down to scoop up their son in love, warmth, and support. They expected Stephen to perform for them, but they never went out of their way to perform for him. They didn't change their plans to include him. They didn't stop what they were doing to notice him, compliment him, or make him feel important. They just hired another babysitter to make sure the details of the child care were tended to. When Stephen was eleven, his father was being honored at a dinner to celebrate his contribution to a big community project. Mom and Dad ordered Stephen to attend in his new blue suit and tie, cementing the image of a perfect family. They didn't even blink at Stephen's disappointment at missing his best friend's birthday party that night. On some sad level, deep inside, down where Stephen had learned to stuff his feelings of not belonging and not being important, he wasn't really surprised. He'd already learned the painful message that he didn't matter and that the world revolved around his parents. Honor was a one-way street in this family. Like honey pouring from a jar, it flowed from Stephen to his parents, but not back the other way. They were celebrities; they counted and he didn't; they were a big deal and he was no deal at all. His biggest value was to make them look good. At those special times he felt a distorted sense of belonging, but most of the time he felt like a misfit. When appearances mattered, Stephen mattered. Otherwise, he belonged to no one.

The problem with Stephen's parents was that they thought more about themselves than about their son. They were self-centered but not child centered. They planned meticulously for their own activities, but if they made a plan around Stephen, it usually blew up in smoke before the event took place. Their only response was an offhanded, casual apology that conveyed to Stephen that they believed their lives were much more important than his and that it was inconsequential to them to disappoint their son. His parents were totally predictable. It was almost guaranteed that they wouldn't do anything special for Stephen because he wasn't on their radar.

Stephen needed to feel accepted. He longed to fit in somewhere. He yearned to feel that he belonged. Since it didn't seem possible to get his needs met in his family, he began to look elsewhere. He soon found what he was looking for—acceptance—in a group of young teenage boys who had started to drink. He knew a lot about alcohol because his parents drank, and he had already begun to raid their liquor cabinet to numb his loneliness. At last he'd found a place where he could fit.

Stephen's newfound "family" drank on weekends, and Stephen found himself stumbling home drunk most of these weekend nights. It worked perfectly for him because his parents weren't accustomed to paying much attention to him anyway, so his behavior went unnoticed for a long time.

One weekend, under the influence, Stephen and his new friends decided to go joyriding. They hot-wired a car, intending to drive it around for a few miles and return it, but they were stopped by the police for a burned-out headlight. Caught red-handed, they were hauled off to the local jail. As each boy told his story and was allowed to make his phone call, parents began to arrive. They talked with the police, began to make arrangements for upcoming legal proceedings, and then took their sons home. Stephen's parents didn't show up. Not because they wanted to teach him a lesson, but because they were disgusted with their failure of a son and his stupid behavior and didn't want to inconvenience themselves in the middle of the night for him.

Stephen paid the legal consequences for the joyriding, and he paid them alone. On the day he went to court, his parents were at a business meeting out of town, so a neighbor drove him to the courthouse. Once more, Mom and Dad proved to their son that they didn't really care. It was blatantly evident to Stephen that he was on his own. His parents were too self-absorbed to bother themselves with Stephen's problems, his feelings, or his life. They never established a meaningful relationship that didn't revolve around them.

After the day in court, when Stephen's parents returned home, they grounded him, a rather antiseptic punishment that didn't require any time or effort on the part of his parents. There was no conversation about what he'd done or why, and no visible involvement with, or concern for, Stephen. They followed a disconnected sense of parental responsibility to do their duty and penalize unacceptable behavior without getting their own hands dirty. Since they relegated the particulars of the grounding to the nanny, they didn't even have to inconvenience themselves in making sure Stephen followed the rules of his punishment. Even in discipline, there was no intimate connection or emotional interaction that made Stephen feel as if he was an important member of the family, or that he and his parents belonged together. At every step of the way, his parents did the things that were socially acceptable on the surface, but they remained disengaged.

As Stephen's teenage years wore on, he became more and more deeply involved in alcohol, then in drugs, the mechanism by which he chose to numb his feelings of nonacceptance and not belonging. He wasn't able to find his niche in his own family, so he clung more and more tenaciously to his group of friends. Only with them could he begin to feel the sense of importance and value he had so desperately longed for from his family, but the group's influence wreaked havoc on Stephen in another way because their main connection was not love and support but rather alcohol and drugs. They weren't trying to help each other get ahead in life and succeed, their bond was in getting drunk and stoned together. Without even realizing it, by the time he graduated from high school, Stephen had become addicted to alcohol and cocaine.

The next ten years of Stephen's life were a mess. He started college but dropped out because he couldn't balance studying with using drugs. Because he had family money, he was able to rent a house, and he worked from time to time at menial jobs. He dated dysfunctional women because no one who was functioning well wanted to be around his chaos for too long. He chose friends by their willingness to kowtow to his money. That way they wouldn't call him on his crazy behavior, and he could feel in control. At last his charade fell apart and he sought help. At AA meetings he learned sobriety, stability, and the value of at last belonging to a group of people who cared about him as a person and accepted him as he was. In therapy we worked on resolving his childhood pain of never belonging, on building genuine self-esteem for the first time, and on choosing a lifestyle that would bring him fulfillment.

We worked on it, but we didn't fix it, because it's almost impossible to eradicate someone's past. When Stephen left therapy, he had turned a corner but still had a long way to go. What happened to him during his childhood was so powerful in determining the direction, shape, and quality of his life that it will take Stephen years to heal. In fact, during his lifetime he'll probably never really heal completely because the message of not belonging is so deeply embedded in his psyche. Sadly, his was an emotional injury so serious that it will be very difficult to recover from it. Unless Stephen does recover, change, and grow, he'll tend to parent his own children exactly as he was parented himself, perpetuating the legacy of disengagement.

Stephen's parents probably never realized what they'd done to damage their son because they never understood that the most important things they could have given him were not things money could buy, but rather their acceptance and approval. What he really needed when he was growing up was a family where he fit in, a place to feel he belonged, a place where he felt important and valued, and a relationship with his parents.

This kind of devastating oversight in parenting happens in varying degrees in many families from one end of the socioeconomic scale to the other. It doesn't just happen in wealthy families or poor families. It's not restricted to white-collar families or blue-collar families. It's common in two-parent families, single-parent families, and gay and straight families. It happens whether one, two, or no parents work out-side the home. Since disengaged parents are everywhere, I believe it's our moral duty to make a greater effort to acknowledge our kids and to give them a secure sense of acceptance and importance.

Parenting is a *contact* sport. You can't do it from a distance or in a disconnected way. You have to be ready to roll up your sleeves and get your hands dirty. To give your kids that all-important sense of belong-ing, you have to get personally involved—you have to be willing to get your feet wet.

You can't delegate your parenting to a nanny, an aunt, or a close friend. I don't mean you can't have help, but you can't give away your responsibility to parent your kids. You know, in all the years I've done therapy, not one client has come to see me for unresolved issues with a babysitter, an uncle, or a neighbor, but dozens and dozens—probably hundreds—have come to work out leftover pain and hurt with their parents. We owe it to our kids to accept them for who they are, to help them feel worthy, and to give them a sense of belonging.

> PARENTING IS A CONTACT SPORT. YOU CAN'T DO IT FROM A DISTANCE OR IN A DISCONNECTED WAY. YOU HAVE TO BE READY TO ROLL UP YOUR SLEEVES AND GET YOUR HANDS DIRTY.

Creating Roots

There are so many ways to give children the sense of belonging and acceptance that makes them feel they're part of a team. Many of those ways are intangible, but a home is often a concrete symbol. When I think of my childhood home, warm memories rush over me. Not because the house itself was so great but because of how loved my mom and dad made me feel there. It was the feelings, not the house, that made me feel like an important part of my family.

The day Carol moved her bedroom to our downstairs apartment, she had some misgivings about forfeiting her traditional place with us upstairs. Although she was excited to be further away from us and more autonomous, it felt strange, at first, to give up that space where she'd belonged for so many years. After she moved her things in and decorated it to suit her taste, the new room quickly became hers. Then she was off to college. Soon thereafter, we decided to reconfigure and remodel the upstairs and turn Carol's new bedroom apartment into my therapy office so I could work at home. In one fell swoop she was about to lose both bedrooms in our house. It was then that I thought of my own childhood bedroom, painted a soft lavender and filled with all the things that were only mine. Even curled up alone in my bed, I remember feeling very much a part of my family there. Knowing our decision to remodel would surely have an emotional impact on Carol, I called her at college. We had a long conversation about bedrooms, home, and belonging, which made both of us realize that home is far more than just a place, and belonging is a terribly significant aspect of family.

Carol agreed with our decision to convert and rebuild, but one question remained to be answered: "Mom, will I still have a place at home?" My answer was quick and easy: "You, my love, always have a place in my home, no matter how big or small. No matter how many bedrooms, no matter what city or even what country I live in. You have that place because home is where our heartfelt relationship has been built, not where the structure of the house is. We are united in our hearts, not in a building."

A family home can give roots, but the more enduring roots grow from the heart, not from the house. That's why creating happy family memories is so important. We definitely had our share, many of which we recorded on film. For Carol's twenty-first birthday I wanted to give her something exceptional, something more unique than money could buy. I spent hours and hours shuffling and sorting through old photographs, picking out my favorites. Each and every photo carried with it a memory of some special event or activity, depicting an unforgettable moment in my mind. I had them put together into a video set to music. It was called "Remembering 21 Years." It was a tender and emotional twenty minutes when we sat together in front of her TV in her college apartment. We watched her life roll by in three-second frames, while tears of sentimentality streamed down my face. Two years later, for Andrea's twenty-first birthday I did the same thing for her. These two videos are very precious to us. Periodically, Terry and I still pull up our chairs in front of the TV so we don't miss a single detail as we watch and cry. He's even worse than I am, considering that he wasn't even around for the first fourteen or so years of their lives. I'm sure there's no doubt in their minds that they belong to him.

A team can never get too big, and it's a joyful event to continue to include more members as children grow up, marry, and have children of their own. As parents and grandparents we have the distinct privilege of continuing to grow, support, and nurture our family ties so that the feeling of belonging becomes our legacy.

Dear Carol and Andrea,

Telling the truth has always been important to me. If I could have chosen only one characteristic for the two of you to develop as kids, I would have picked honesty.

In fact, I explicitly told you when you were young that I would go out on a limb to support you, defend you, even fight for you, but if I ever found out you had lied to me, it would change the nature of our relationship dramatically. I would go to the nth degree for you as long as I knew I could trust you to tell me the truth, but once that trust was broken, it would take a long time to build it back.

I know it must have been really hard for you at times. I'm sure you had to muster up all the courage you had inside you and then take a deep breath before blurting out the truth to me. But what a payoff—to have always known we could trust each other.

I love you bushels and nightgowns,

Mom

6

The Courage to Spill the Beans:

Fostering a Family Culture of Honesty

O F ALL THE CHARACTER TRAITS I tried to teach my two daughters, there is one that stands head and shoulders above the rest. Telling the truth isn't just a moral thing to do, it's also a psychologically healthy thing to do. It sets you free and allows you to be who you are. In contrast, hiding, lying, and sneaking cause enormous stress and bind you up inside. You have to use excessive energy to keep your stories straight and your bases covered. This is as true for kids as it is for adults. If we help our children learn to tell the truth when they're young, it helps to develop the character trait of honesty for a lifetime. Likewise, if we allow dishonesty in our children, it promotes dishonesty into adulthood.

Years ago a client, Kimberly, came to see me because she knew she lied whenever it seemed easier than telling the truth. She'd become so accustomed to saying what she thought other people wanted to hear that she'd developed huge anxiety, thinking of the multiple interpretations of the same event she'd given to different people. Kimberly knew she couldn't be trusted and worried that others were treating her as dishonestly as she was treating them. Her habit was so long standing that she was afraid she'd never be able to turn it around and learn to be truthful again. Her self-esteem had plummeted because she was regularly violating her own value system. She'd damaged friendships as well as her self-worth one lie at a time. It was a long and difficult road back toward telling the truth and living at a level acceptable to herself.

TRUST AND TRUTH GO TOGETHER, AND IT'S EITHER ALL OR NOTHING. IF YOU DON'T TELL THE TRUTH ALL OF THE TIME, THEN YOU AREN'T TRUSTWORTHY, BECAUSE NO ONE EVER KNOWS WHEN YOU'RE BEING HONEST AND WHEN YOU'RE NOT.

Trust and truth go together, and it's either all or nothing. If you don't tell the truth all of the time, then you aren't trustworthy, because no one ever knows when you're being honest and when you're not. When I think about my own friends and the people I've known in my life, I realize that the ones whom I trust to tell me the truth are the ones with whom I've developed meaningful relationships. These are the relationships that last a lifetime. In contrast, the people I couldn't trust have fallen by the wayside, or at least they've taken up a position on the periphery where I feel they can't betray me or harm me. Likewise, if there isn't honesty between parents and their children, there won't be trust or closeness in the family either.

Obviously, no one tells his or her parents absolutely everything. We all have, and are entitled to have, a private life—our thoughts and feelings, the intimate behaviors we save for our partners, the very personal things we hold close to our hearts. Your kids don't have to tell you everything, but your goal should be to create an environment where they *want* to talk with you about their lives and feel safe that you won't judge or punish them for what they share.

Many years ago Matthew came to see me for therapy. As we talked about his relationship with his dad, Matthew told me how judgmental his dad was. As a result, Matthew always tried to please him and get his approval. One day Matthew told me a story from when he was eight years old. He had been playing with paints in the backyard when his friend dared him to swipe the neighbors' white picket fence with blue paint. Of course, everyone in the neighborhood noticed, including Matthew's dad. When Dad confronted Matthew, he denied it. But Dad noticed the paint on his son's hands. Matthew was caught blue-handed. When I asked Matthew why he couldn't tell his dad the truth, he said he was too scared and didn't want to disappoint his father by admitting to his mistake. His dad had not created an environment that made it safe for Matthew to be honest. Instead of asking about the facts and exploring with his son why he would have done such a thing, Matthew's dad simply punished him soundly. Punishment may have been appropriate, but they also should have talked. Because they didn't, Matthew felt even less safe to share his mistakes with his dad in the future.

Lots of Opportunities

While your kids are growing up, you have many opportunities to help them learn to be honest. Sometimes the lessons are about lies of commission. (You may ask, "Did you go to the basketball game last night?" And your daughter answers, "Yes, I did," when, actually, she did not. Instead she spent the evening at a friend's house. She told a lie—a lie of *commission*.) Other times the lessons are about lies of omission. (You ask, "What did you do last night?" Your son replies, "I hung out at Derek's house." That part's true, but he omitted telling you that, later, they went to a party at the house of a friend whose parents were out of town. In neglecting to tell you the whole truth—something he knows you would want to know—he tells a lie of *omission*.)

Getting kids to tell the truth can be complicated, but it's an important job for parents because honesty is not a trait that necessarily develops naturally. Just like so many other characteristics you'd like your kids to have, this one depends a lot on you. Often kids want to come clean. But it takes courage. It's certainly easier to simply omit the parts they think you'll freak out over. It's your responsibility to make it possible for them *not* to give you lies of omission. Carol taught me that lesson many years ago.

GETTING KIDS TO TELL THE TRUTH CAN BE COMPLICATED, BUT IT'S AN IMPORTANT JOB FOR PARENTS BECAUSE HONESTY IS NOT A TRAIT THAT NECESSARILY DEVELOPS NATURALLY.

It was an otherwise ordinary Saturday night, just before spring break during Carol's senior year of high school. Except that she blew it, and she blew it big. She'd gone out with friends and ended up at a keg party where she drank too much beer, tripped over the keg, and broke her nose. A sober friend drove her home. As usual, she woke us up to tell us she was home, and then dropped into bed. No confessions that night. When morning came, she had two black eyes, a sore nose, and a defeated spirit. She promptly came forth with the entire story, no details omitted. More than anything, we felt sorry for her. A story like hers would remind most parents of their own youths and the old adage about not throwing stones when you live in a glass house. It didn't mean we approved of her behavior, but it did put it in perspective and make it more difficult to get angry.

Carol had to have surgery and wear a drip pad under her nose for several days. The kids at school were all abuzz with poor Carol's misfortune. It was too good of a story not to talk about. All the teachers asked her what happened, so she had to respond to their probing questions as well. When doctor's orders prohibited her from joining her friends in the desert over spring break for a camping trip, she was devastated, and playing soccer for her final spring at high school was out. She paid a high price for her misjudgment. The world around her punished Carol more effectively than I ever could have, so I used the opportunity to show her my compassion, talk about the ramifications of drinking, and appreciate her for being honest with me.

Although all her friends knew exactly what had happened, no one ever mentioned a word of it to me. She could have lied and made up a whole different story about how she broke her nose. I probably would never have found out, but she chose to take the high road and honor our relationship. She chose to value our mutual trust and tell the truth.

Years later I asked Carol *why* she had chosen to tell me the truth about her broken nose. She said I had already proven to her that I would not humiliate her or be unreasonable. In some way she welcomed the opportunity to get it off her chest so she could be relieved of her guilt and confirm that she was still a good person in spite of her stupid mistake. She didn't want to carry a secret inside her—she never wanted to lie to me—because she knew it would hurt our relationship. She also said that because I treated her with compassion and fairness when she broke her nose, she realized she could trust me to tell me the truth in the future.

Sometimes kids *want* to get caught so they can feel renewed to start again, and parents need to make it safe for kids to fess up. It's tough for kids to tell the truth, especially if they think they're going to be disciplined for their misconduct. As parents, we should be sure to provide a benefit by showing our understanding and by telling them how much we respect them for making their courageous confession.

Andrea also learned not to tell lies of omission. When she was just fourteen, she wanted to go with Carol on an overnight trip to Vail to watch the boys' soccer team play. Of course, she wanted to go because her boyfriend was playing. Carol was sixteen, had her driver's license, and had made plans to drive over with a couple of girlfriends. My concern with Andrea was that she always wanted to do things that were just a little bit too old for her, but this time, right or wrong, I allowed her to go. We went over every possible situation that might come up for her and discussed how she should respond and behave in every case. Then I crossed my fingers and watched them all drive away together. When they returned home two days later, Andrea was totally up front and honest. She told me every detail about what had happened and everything she'd done, including going into the hot tub at the hotel with a group of the soccer boys. She'd worn a T-shirt and shorts. As I visibly cringed at the mental image of my daughter in a wet T-shirt, sitting in a frothy Jacuzzi with a group of teenage boys, she defended herself by reminding me that she hadn't taken a bathing suit.

I hadn't thought to prohibit that particular activity—you can't think of every single one! She hadn't disobeyed, but more important, she did not omit telling me the things she knew I'd want to know.

Although I didn't condone the behavior, from then on I knew I could trust her to be truthful with me and not give me lies of omission.

Teaching Them Honesty

When kids are young, four principles make it easier for them to tell the truth. Following are the four principles:
- Don't judge or ridicule
- Model honesty
- Use moments of truth telling to teach
- Be firm on honesty, tender on your kids

These principles make telling the truth something that supports and affirms your relationship with your kids, and they help you keep your confidence in your children no matter what.

Honesty Principle #1: Don't Judge or Ridicule

One time Andrea came home an hour later than we'd agreed upon. When I confronted her, she admitted that she was actually home on time but had been outside in the car kissing her boyfriend. I stayed calm and responded, "Well, I know that can be fun, but I expect you to honor your word and be home on time." She never did it again. Why not? Because she was a Goody Two-shoes? Not at all! She told me recently that she could tell me the truth because she never feared me. She trusted that I'd be compassionate, not sneer at her or harshly criticize her. In that instance, Andrea remembered that I hadn't been angry but that I had called her on it, and because she valued our relationship, she did it only once.

If you judge kids, laugh at them, or sling recriminations rather than honor their mistakes, kids won't open up. If you're unpredictable or inconsistent, they'll be afraid to share with you. And remember my tip that when a problem arises, don't panic. You can still discipline them for unacceptable behavior by involving them in a discussion about it and allowing them to participate in setting consequences. Make your discipline about interaction and the opportunity for them to learn so that kids understand the reasoning in it. They'll notice the difference between discipline, in which they participate, and punishment, which is beyond their control. Punishment doesn't invite either discussion or learning—it's something that's done *to* you and it damages the relationship rather than builds it. Your kids will respect you for your wisdom in being fair, and it will make it easier for them to be honest with you.

Honesty Principle #2: Model Honesty

Because honesty was so huge for me, I knew I had to model for Carol and Andrea not only truthful words but also a truthful lifestyle. I could hardly expect to teach them honesty by living a secret life and lying to them. That meant I disclosed certain things about my life that I might otherwise have kept from them. For example, after I was divorced, I shared my thoughts about the men I went out with. Not the inappropriate or intimate details, but my feelings, as well as the things I was learning about myself and the dating world. Rather than having a hidden or secret life, I wanted my life to be an open book. If I wanted them to tell me the truth about their lives, I knew I would have to tell them the truth about mine. So, as the issues came up and as the timing was appropriate, I openly told them everything I could think of about myself. They heard all my childhood infractions, my dating experiences, stories about boyfriends, the times I tried drugs, stupid things I did while traveling, tales of their dad and me. I didn't share with them my most personal life, but I kept no secrets from them. I wanted them to know the truth about who I was.

Perhaps the hardest truth I ever told them came the summer after their dad and I separated. Andrea was nine and Carol was eleven. We were hiking over the weekend to a beautiful lake in the mountains and had stopped to look at the spectacular view when the question came.

"Was Daddy ever unfaithful to you?" Andrea asked.

I stammered, I stuttered, I hesitated, I avoided, and then I changed the subject without addressing her question.

Monday morning I raced to the counseling center where I'd started working and asked a couple of colleagues for advice. This is what they said: "Always tell the truth. If they're asking the question, it's probably because they already know the answer and want confirmation for what they already know in their hearts. Don't confuse the issue by lying, even if you think it's a white lie; don't elaborate on the answer by going into details they don't want or need to know. Simply answer the question truthfully and move on.

"In addition," my colleagues added, "if they really want to know, they'll ask you again."

About two weeks later the girls and I were all on the deck outside our family room when Andrea asked the question again. This time, strengthened by the advice of my fellow therapists, I took a deep breath and gave my one-word answer.

Neither of them asked any more questions, and the matter was settled for several years. I was glad to have answered their question honestly, and I further cemented the habit of telling the truth in our family, even when it's hard.

In my therapy practice, I've had numerous couples over the years who have hidden their drug usage from their kids. They knew it was wrong, and they realized it would be a negative influence on their kids, so they did it on the sneak. The question I've always asked these couples is, "Why would you expect your children to be honest with you if you're lying to them?" Every time you lie to your children, you give them a subtle message that you don't value honesty in your family. Every time a parent or a child lives a lie, it erodes the emotional health of the family. In AA they say it's your secrets that keep you sick. That axiom applies to families as well.

Honesty Principle #3: Use Moments of Truth Telling to Teach

One day Carol and I were doing errands together when she blurted out that she had drunk alcohol for the first time at a party the night before. It was a year or so prior to her keg-party incident. She was sixteen and had spent the night with a group of friends at another friend's home. I was surprised to hear that her friend's mom had poured the wine for all of them.

I'd always wondered how I'd react the first time either of my kids reported that news to me. I'd made a decision many years before, and, thankfully, it popped into my mind: *In a moment of surprise or a time of crisis, do not react.* First and foremost, be sure to keep contact—protect and secure the relationship, not saying anything that would judge, ridicule, or scold in such a way that would close down communication, sever trust, or jam a wedge in the relationship. There's plenty of time to talk about the issue at hand, but if you shut down your child with an inappropriate burst at the beginning, you lose the opportunity to talk, teach, and guide. So, the only thing that came forth when Carol confessed to drinking was, "I always wondered how I'd react the first time you told me that you drank."

For Carol it was a monumental moment of telling the truth because she didn't omit what she knew I wanted to know, even though I'd never have found out if she hadn't offered the information. On my part, punishment didn't seem right; getting angry didn't seem right; lecturing didn't seem right. Whenever I didn't know what to do, I defaulted to a relationship position and talked with her. That felt right. In addition, it seemed like the perfect opportunity to teach her some things about drinking. I started with several questions that we discussed to stimulate her thinking about alcohol and her own behaviors. She'd had small amounts of wine with us at home, but never on her own. How did it feel? What did she like about it? What about the peer pressure, and how did her friends react to her drinking? How much did she drink? Did she want to drink more? Did she think she'd do it again? Why did she tell me? How did she think I'd react? I knew I couldn't prevent her from drinking, but as long as we were honest and respectful with each other, and as long as I didn't slam her with judgment and punishment every time she shared something about her life, I figured I'd have the best shot at helping her make better decisions for herself.

Honesty Principle #4: Be Firm on Honesty, Tender on Your Kids

Honesty also includes subjects such as stealing and sneaking out of the house. When Carol was quite young, Andrea ratted on her. Andrea said that Carol had shoplifted a pack of gum from the grocery store. Although I'm not a big fan of tattling, I asked Carol if it was true. Bless her heart. Her eyes looked so guilty and her small voice trembled as she confessed her deed. There was no lecture, no punishment. I thought she would learn her lesson better by dealing with the actual consequences of her shoplifting than being given a generic punishment. But I was not willing to let this small infraction slide by because it could have led to larger ones. We simply hopped in the car and drove back to the grocery store. I found the manager and stood silently by Carol's side while she quietly and fearfully handed him the gum and explained what she'd done. The lesson she learned was very powerful, and it taught her that I put more stock in honesty than in punishment. As a bystander, Andrea was also impacted by her sister's actions. That day they both took another giant leap forward in telling the truth.

Everyone has the ability to be honest, but if you don't practice it, then you may develop the habit of cutting corners, fudging, and telling white lies—because it's easier. As a parent, you have the opportunity to help your children develop the characteristic of being honest, but it has to be nurtured. Don't lower your standards, but do understand that they won't be perfect. Remember that total honesty is difficult, because most of us have a secret or two lurking in the closet.

What Would You Do?

Recently, my longtime friend Sandy told me about an intense period in her life several years ago. Her story grabbed my heart because it could have happened in any family.

When Sandy's daughter Nicole was in college, she called her mom early one morning as Sandy was just getting up. Nicole stammered and hesitated, then blurted out that she was pregnant. Sandy's response could have been: "You're what? I can't believe this! Now what are you going to do? You've really messed up your life this time, and you've disappointed me more than you can even imagine!"

Or her mom could have said: "Oh, sweetie, I love you. Now, don't worry. We'll talk and we'll figure it out. It will be okay."

Which way would you respond if you were the mom? Thank goodness, Sandy responded the second way.

DON'T LOWER YOUR STANDARDS, BUT DO UNDERSTAND THAT THEY WON'T BE PERFECT.

During her junior year, Nicole had spent a semester studying in Europe. It was a confusing period in her life. She was struggling with her own identity issues and was trying to find her place in the social scene. She'd been a late bloomer and didn't quite know how to relate to guys yet. For a variety of reasons, she was not good at setting her own boundaries, so it was hard for her to say no, hard to draw the line between what she wanted to do for herself and what others wanted her to do for them.

You can probably guess what happened. Away from home, in a different culture, with fewer clear-cut regulations than normal, Nicole met a young local man. She was with him for only a couple of weeks, but in those two weeks, he made her feel like a queen. It's pretty hard to resist a guy who showers you with attention, and it's pretty seductive when he tells you all the things you've been dying to hear for a long time. He disappeared as quickly as he appeared. Nicole went to the same places they'd spent time in and tried to find the couple of friends she knew he had, but she never saw him again. For the next few days, she felt devastated, as wretched as she had felt glorious. Gradually, she put it all in perspective and began to realize it had been a fun fling that was now over.

Until the time when her next period should have come. The first day Nicole was perplexed, the second anxious, the third scared, and from then on terrified. She felt all alone in a world she knew nothing about; she only knew she wasn't ready for this. She didn't know what to do or where to turn, so she tried to put it out of her mind.

Within a month, Nicole's semester abroad was over and she returned home. By now she was nearly a walking zombie, trying to show excitement about her European adventures but feeling frantic inside. On the one hand, she trusted her mom more than anyone else in the world. On the other hand, she was afraid to tell her. Up until then, she had always revealed her secrets to her mom, sharing with her a variety of escapades she'd had in high school and college. Although her mom had not always agreed with Nicole, she'd been predictably understanding. Her mom had long since proven herself to be a wise and reasoned confidante for Nicole. Of course, pregnancy had never been on the table before. This was a monumental issue of mammoth proportions and enormous ramifications. Could she possibly trust her mom enough on this one to tell her the truth and ask for help? Finally, she gathered up all her courage and called her mom. Nicole hadn't wanted to tell her because she didn't want to disappoint or hurt her, but she was the only person Nicole trusted with this crisis in her life.

As they talked on the phone, Sandy tried to soothe Nicole and give her the long-distance hugs she so desperately needed. They began to explore avenues and make plans together. Within a couple of days, Nicole's mom and dad were on a plane. They spent the weekend together as a family, formulating the next steps of the process they would go through.

Several days later, Nicole admitted that her mom was the person she wanted most to talk to in her time of great confusion, pain, and need. She felt guilty that she'd underestimated her mom's instant serenity and calmness, her immediate attention to Nicole's terror, her ability to think so clearly and logically, and her overall umbrella of love and compassion. Most of all, Nicole was grateful that she felt absolutely no judgment or criticism from her mom. Of course, her mom told me that that was the easy part because there *was* no judgment or criticism. Sandy had thought back to her own youth and a few stupid and unthinking moments she'd had with guys in her own life. She could remember how fortunate she was not to have found herself in the same kind of predicament her daughter was now in.

Even a great, truthful relationship with your kids doesn't prevent problems. It's not necessarily intended to. It *is* intended to cement a strong bond between you so that whatever your kids go through, you get to go through it with them.

Parent-child relationships are very powerful, and that makes it even harder for kids to tell parents the truth. Kids—at any age—seem to have an innate fear of disappointing or hurting their parents. Even a good relationship doesn't necessarily make it easy to share your problems, but it *does* make it possible. That makes it even more essential for us parents and stepparents to maintain an open and intimate connection with our kids so that we're accessible to them whenever they need us. Parenting begins long before birth. I'm clear about that. But how long does it last? According to my experiences with my own daughters and my therapy clients, and confirmed by Nicole's experience with her parents, it's evident that parenting never stops. It evolves and changes over time. Roles shift, discipline disappears, and power equalizes, but the relationship lasts forever. The more open and honest that relationship is, the greater the friendship and the greater the healthy involvement in each other's lives. Even as kids grow into adults, it feels great to have the support of a close family that's grounded in telling the truth.

Dear Carol and Andrea,

I admit it. The two things that scared me most during your teenage years were sex and drugs—barring any catastrophic accident or illness, of course. With your hormones in full  swing, your feelings passionate, and the peer pressure intense, there was rarely a dull moment.

It's ironic that the more fun you were having—partying, hanging out with boys, and staying out late—the more frightened I got!

I can't wait until you each go through this with your own kids. It's bound to give you at least a few gray hairs.

I love you bushels and nightgowns,

Mom

CHAPTER 7

It's Pretty Funny when You're Six:

Teaching Your Kids About Sex, Drugs, and Rock 'n' Roll

NO DOUBT EVERY FAMILY FACES A SERIES of challenges as their kids are growing up. Some challenges are inherent parts of children learning to be adults, but others stem from the world around kids: their communities, their schools, and all the other environments they're enveloped in. New predicaments bombard our lives on a regular basis, and young people are constantly experimenting. The way families deal with all of these challenges depends upon their belief systems, their comfort with talking among themselves, and their relationship with one another. The more parents understand their own beliefs, the more they feel at ease talking with their kids and teaching them family values. The stronger their relationships, the easier it is to handle every one of these challenges.

Each family has its own rules and rituals to steer a moral path through the minefields of modern life. I've often been impressed with the clever and thoughtful ways parents have taught their kids about kindness, sharing, and treating others with respect. Sometimes they feel confused or uninformed, so they've come to see me for counseling on bullying, stealing, or cheating. But the issues that give them the most nightmares—the ones that freeze most parents—are the most inevitable of all: sex, drugs, and rock 'n' roll.

Over the years, I've done a lot of drug and alcohol counseling. One of my saddest clients was referred to me by his employer. This clients' drug of choice was alcohol. He worked in the kitchen of a local restaurant, and his employer was generously giving him another chance by paying for his therapy and offering him payment and a leave of absence to attend a thirty-day treatment program. I saw this client only twice.

The first time, he came to my office downtrodden and depressed. He didn't have much to say because he was deeply entrenched in his alcohol addiction. He was physically ill and he felt hopeless, but he'd been drinking for so many years he couldn't envision life without it. I spent most of the hour explaining the characteristics and progression of the disease of alcoholism. I talked with him about the new hope for his life if he would only avail himself of his employer's offer and check into a treatment center. At the end of the session he thanked me and walked out, head down and shoulders bent.

The second time I saw him he was lying in a hospital bed. His employer had called to tell me that the man had been hospitalized for severe liver problems and was told he wouldn't live unless he quit drinking. When I walked into his room he just looked at me. I tried to be gentle and encouraging, recommending again that he agree to treatment. I offered support and therapy as soon as he returned, trying once more to give him hope to rebuild his life. But he couldn't make the commitment.

His employer told me later that the man had been released from the hospital, but he died shortly thereafter. A sad ending to a sad life. I never learned a lot about this poor man, but I did know that he was lonely, with no one to talk to. He didn't have people in his life who cared about him, included him, or made him feel valuable. I can't help but believe he learned to numb his feelings and drown his sorrows in alcohol.

When the thoughts and curiosities about sex, drugs, and rock 'n' roll come tumbling into your kids' lives, no one has a more significant role to play than you, their parents. Not only in making them feel precious, cared about, and loved, but also in teaching them what it's all about.

> **THE ISSUES THAT FREEZE MOST PARENTS ARE THE MOST INEVITABLE OF ALL: SEX, DRUGS, AND ROCK 'N' ROLL.**

Sex: Start Talking Early

Our first family conversations about sex began quite easily because Carol and Andrea were both young, so young that they didn't even know we were talking about sex. Because we had started nurturing a relationship of trust and openness so early on, when they grew old enough to begin to understand, it was already as normal as apple pie.

We started in the bathroom, not having a major discussion, but just being in the same space together when I was taking care of my monthly business. You can imagine a few of their early questions: "What's that thing, Mommy?" "Where are you sticking it?" "Why?" "How often do you do that?" These all promoted some rich explanations that constructed the springboard for talks about sex.

When we were all comfortable and informed about healthy bodily functions, the girls were ready to bounce into a lot of different directions, each one requiring a simple, totally normal explanation about sperm, egg, womb, pregnancy, birth—anything and everything.

It's not, "Okay, my precious child. It's time to have The Talk about the birds and bees" (gulp, stammer, hesitate, blurt). Rather, it can be a series of much more casual talks or explanations extended over years and meant to answer their normal, curious questions. Each talk may be only a sentence long. Or it may briefly answer the naïve question your children ask. The older they get and the more curious they become, the more detailed and comprehensive the explanations can be. If you start having these conversations when your children are little, it's about as scary or embarrassing as explaining how to can tomatoes.

I didn't keep a journal then, so I don't remember precise ages or exact facts, but I do recall one incident when Andrea was six years old. We were at a resort with another couple who also had kids the same ages. One afternoon Andrea and Carol returned from playing with their little friends in their condo, and Andrea was atwitter with excited news and breathless questions.

"Mommy, Erica and I were playing and I heard some funny noises. I went to the bedroom door and peeked through the crack, and Mommy, Erica's daddy was on top of her mommy, and he was sort of going up and down and they were both making these funny noises. Mommy, what were they doing?"

Take a deep breath. Let that little incident sink in and seize the moment. By age six, Andrea knew lots of things about sex, but she did not know how the sperm and the egg got together. She'd never asked, so I figured she hadn't been ready to know. Maybe this was the time. I began a very calm and reasoned explanation of exactly how that sperm and that egg made contact, couched in the context of how God planned this as a way for a husband and a wife who loved each other very much to experience pleasure and make babies at the same time. As the nuances rolled out, her big, eight-year-old sister stood smugly to the side, a pleased look of already knowing spread all over her face. Then Andrea began to cradle her little arms in front of her and squish up her small face into a widespread grin.

"Why are you smiling so big?" I asked. "It's the plan God thought up. It's not really funny."

She instantly quipped, "It's pretty funny when you're six!"

Well, I suppose. I'll give her that. Now that she knew it all, we were set to have any and every conversation from then on—and we did.

As an addendum, it took me a few years to share this with my mortified friend, Erica's mom. She hadn't closed the door securely and was horrified to have been so negligent. I assured her that Andrea had not been psychologically damaged, and it was really a fortunate moment for us. It has even become one of those reminiscent moments for laughter among all of us.

Most families aren't likely to have a friend who physically demonstrates a sexual act for their kids, so they have to look for the right opportunity, the right moment, the right setting to talk about sex and sexuality. It's only a matter of developing the willingness to have this kind of conversation, because sex is all around us.

There are three reasons to talk with your kids about sex:
- To establish a family culture of talking
- To make sure your kids get accurate information
- To counsel and guide your kids

There's no shortage of entrees into the conversation if you have a mental posture of relaxing into it instead of avoiding it.

Reason #1: To Establish a Family Culture of Talking

One of the reasons for all the early conversations is to establish the family culture, build the open and sharing relationship, and set the tone for the conversations that come later. To the credit of my mom and dad, even though they were members of a very strict religion that decried sex and proclaimed that the women who participated in it were the root of all evil, they told me about sex when I was very young. I remember it was a Sunday morning before we all got up to go to church. They invited me to crawl into bed with them—right in the middle between them was my favorite place—and they told me. I don't remember how the conversation went after all these decades, but I think it was pretty matter of fact and straightforward.

I still respect my parents for stepping outside their box back then and doing what probably no other parents in our church, or even in our town, did in those days. Because they were open to talking with me about sex, I was able to ask them questions, and it made me feel closer to them. In middle school we "older" kids spent our recess sitting in a circle at the far end of the playground and telling dirty jokes. Honestly, I didn't understand most of them because I was naïve and the jokes were so corny, but I would silently repeat them in my mind so I could remember to ask my mom or dad at dinner what the jokes meant. (They were so dumb that sometimes my mom and dad couldn't figure them out, either!) For me, it was comforting to know I could talk to my parents about that kind of stuff, and it made me feel closer to them.

Unfortunately, although my parents grabbed the courage to have these early conversations with me, opening the door to deeper and more personal talks about sex and sexuality, they dropped the ball with me when I was older and when it would have been really helpful. The objective lessons about sex are easier, and it takes more courage to talk with your kids about what's actually going on in their own lives. But those continuing, ever-deeper conversations are the ones that steer your kids toward better decision making for themselves. And if you don't have a family culture that supports talking, your kids are left on their own, to talk only with their peers.

Reason #2: To Make Sure Your Kids Get Accurate Information

Believe me, you'd rather have your kids talking to you about this than getting their answers from their peers. For all their posturing, adolescents know less about sex than you think. When our seventeen-year-old foster daughter lived with us, she told me things about sex that had me wondering why every girl in high school hadn't gotten pregnant. Her information wasn't accurate. For example, she tried to assure me that if the boy didn't insert his penis too far inside the girl, there was no chance she could get pregnant.

> YOU'D RATHER HAVE YOUR KIDS TALKING TO YOU ABOUT THIS THAN GETTING THEIR ANSWERS FROM THEIR PEERS.

I definitely wanted my kids to have accurate information. In addition, when they were developing breast buds, beginning to menstruate, and starting to think about boyfriends, they didn't have to check out how I'd react, whether I'd snicker or judge, whether I'd be embarrassed or prudish. They already felt pretty comfortable, I think, to ask me questions and to gather information because this was nothing new to us. When their hormones started racing through their bodies, we could talk reasonably about what was going on, just as we'd been doing for a long time.

My daughters and I talked about different topics at differing levels of depth, at different times in their lives. These conversations were commonplace for us. Nothing was ever outside the parameters because we'd established that kind of a relationship when they'd barely been able to speak in full sentences. But let's not kid ourselves. All the previews are in preparation for the full-length feature, that moment when your children decide to have sex, because that's when they need your advice, your input, and your counsel. Believe it or not, if you have a strong, intimate connection, you can be the one they talk to—and listen to—even about sex.

Reason #3: To Counsel and Guide Your Kids

Andrea started her five-year relationship with Brian when she was fourteen. She told me that she only wanted a boyfriend and hadn't planned to fall in love, but her heart melted for Brian, and fall in love she did. It didn't feel like puppy love or immature passion. It was the real thing, and we all know what comes along with adult love.

I was at a conference when my precious fourteen-year-old dropped the first bomb on the phone to me. In a way, I wasn't surprised. I could see it coming on the horizon, but I was hoping the horizon was about ten or twenty years away. For all our modern thinking, most parents (and especially dads) don't want their daughters to have sex until they're thirty or married, whichever comes last. I had envisioned, with all my great parenting skills, especially instilling my values, that both of my daughters would be virgins when they married.

I thank God for our relationship. That must have been what I meant all those years before when I looked into their little upturned faces and said I wanted to develop something with them stronger than their misguided idea that I had power over them. I must have had a clue that one day they'd decide things for themselves, in spite of all the influence I'd try to exert over them, and no influence would be strong enough to persuade them my way. That's why I wanted a relationship, so that when the power dissipated, we'd have a bond with each other that would hold us together through the hard times.

I sensed immediately that Andrea and I were beginning a hard time. As we talked on the phone that night, I was filled with instant panic. She felt sex was the natural next step in the development of her relationship with Brian. She also realized this was a *big* step. I know she took it very seriously and wanted us to be on the same page before she did anything that could not be reversed. She wanted my permission, my agreement, my sanction. I could give her none of those because she was so young.

My mind was racing, my soul was sad, and my heart was burdened with the thought of Andrea becoming a woman so early. I was frantic. I wanted more than anything to talk her out of it. She was only a child. From my perspective, this road was disaster from the beginning and would only lead to more disaster. Sex at this young age was everything negative and not one thing positive. I asked her to wait until we could talk face to face and she agreed, I think, because we had built this foundation of respect and trust.

A few days after I returned home, Andrea brought it up again. Actually, I was amazed and deeply grateful that she wanted to talk with me. Most kids don't ask permission from their moms before they have sex, but Andrea had always been extraordinary in every way. She just couldn't bring herself to break up our intimate relationship by putting this huge and important secret between us.

I didn't know what to do, but I *did* know that I didn't want to lose Andrea or the amazing relationship we'd been building for the entire fourteen years of her life. More than anything, I wanted to control this situation, I wanted to forbid her, I wanted to make her behave my way. I also realized there was only so much I could do short of tying her up at home! I didn't want to lose her trust, which surely would have closed her off from me, so we just kept talking. In fact, we talked over and over and over and over. Our conversations, as I remember them, were intense but always loving and respectful. Neither of us raised our voices or got angry. We didn't judge or criticize each other. We were both trying to influence the other because it was important for us to be on the same side of the fence. It distressed Andrea to think about blatantly engaging in something I so openly disapproved of. I could feel the fragility of her spirit as she expressed her feelings, her perspectives, and her thoughts with great sincerity. She was firm, she was determined, yet she was ever so soft in her approach to me.

> I WANTED TO CONTROL THIS SITUATION, I WANTED TO FORBID HER, I WANTED TO MAKE HER BEHAVE MY WAY . . . [BUT] I DIDN'T WANT TO LOSE HER TRUST.

My heart went out to Andrea even as I clung to my own beliefs. I wanted nothing more than to be able to give the approval she so desperately sought, but I could not. I know we both carried the burden of our differing opinions like heavy yokes slung over our shoulders because we weren't accustomed to living in disagreement. We both felt drained as we explored this issue together for days and weeks on end. Back and forth we went, as we practiced a verbal and emotional dance with each other. I was aware of what an unusual mother-daughter interplay we were engaged in, and I'm still in wonder all these years later.

I gave every reason I could think of for Andrea not to have sex, and we talked about every aspect of sex I was aware of. Physical disease, birth control, and pregnancy were the simple ones. We also talked about how emotions become entangled and they could obscure her ability to see who her boyfriend really was. It's like hanging a gauzy screen between them. And speaking of emotions, girls get tied in to the relationship in a different way from boys, making it a lot more painful if things don't work out. Sometimes girls feel pressured into having sex, or they believe they can snare a guy if they give in to sex. And, as women, our bodies are being invaded during sex. That's a serious event.

We dove into the issues around Andrea's self-esteem and how easy it is to lose it when you give away what is most precious to you—your body. I shared with her about therapy clients who felt used and abused from giving themselves to multiple guys over time. I shared how many times I'd heard women talk about just sleeping with guys because it was fun, with no thought about how deeply they felt for these guys. It was a perfect time to talk about setting boundaries and saying no. Of course, I was worried about promiscuity, and I talked with her about my desperate fear of her losing her morals and her standards, becoming desensitized to her internal boundaries and allowing sex to become her norm with anyone and everyone who could persuade her.

Then there were our discussions about sex without intimacy, an activity totally different from sex with intimacy. I explained how casual sex can set up a hardness around sex that's difficult to overcome and how many clients I'd seen over the years—both male and female—who'd never experienced sex with intimacy.

Because we value what the Bible has to say about our lives, we reviewed the scripture verses about inappropriate sex. We talked about how the word gets out, how she could become known as the girl who *does,* and how it could affect her reputation. We discussed her age—her very young age—and the idea of losing the innocence of childhood so early.

But these were not one-sided lectures. They were full-on two-sided conversations. I admit I sometimes sounded preachy. I can still feel my desperation to sway her to my way of thinking. I guess I'm incapable of smoothing it out into a pretty story where I looked like the perfect mom. I was terrifyingly afraid that I'd lose this one, that I'd truly lost control of the most important issue in my daughter's life. I thought back to all the times when I'd compromised and let her have her way, hoping it would count for something when we got to the big, important one. Maybe I was wrong, I agonized to myself in private. Maybe this relationship idea was just babble. If I couldn't persuade her to take my advice when the stakes were high, then what good was it to have taken all the trouble to build the relationship? I had no one to talk to except Terry, because I wanted to protect Andrea's privacy. There were no books that I knew of to advise moms on how to deal with a young daughter wanting to have sex. It was a gritty time for me.

I know Andrea felt alone, too, having no one to talk to except me. She cried with me because she wanted my approval against all odds. Although I wasn't making much headway in convincing her to change

her mind, she was eager to hear everything I had to say about the subject. She has always done her research before entering into anything
new, and this was no exception. I respected her greatly for engaging in
our conversations and for hearing me out before she responded. On the
one hand, I was desperate to convince her of my point of view. On the
other hand, I admired her tenacity to stick to her guns and not let the
power of my position sway her. She listened intently to what I had to say
and remained open to hearing each of my points, considering them and
evaluating them genuinely. She disagreed, but she was logical. She
defended herself and she explained how she felt and believed. She was
unbelievably mature. All these years I've kept an old, tan suede shirt
stained on the left shoulder with Andrea's tears from that period. From
time to time, I've taken out the shirt to look at those stains, which
remind me of the tenderness of this time we shared so many years ago.

So we talked, but Andrea's never been easily dissuaded. She wanted to be safe, she wanted to see a doctor, and she wanted me to go with
her to the appointment. She pleaded with me to endorse this act. We
cried together as I assured her that I would always love her no matter
what, but I couldn't condone her behavior. She and her sister knew me
better than anyone else on earth. They knew that it was not within me
to approve. Since giving my blessing to this wouldn't have been consistent with who I was, it would have been confusing to them if I'd done it.
If I'd given my sanction, it would have been contrary to everything they
knew about me. Andrea wouldn't expect me to change my whole belief
system based on a situation between her and her boyfriend. If I did, it
would make me unreliable in her mind and her sister's. Then they
wouldn't really be able to depend on me for judgment or wisdom
because they'd know that, under pressure, I had bent my belief system.

WHAT WE NEEDED TO DO HERE, I WAS FINALLY REALIZING, WAS NOT TO CHANGE THE OTHER PERSON, BUT TO ACCEPT EACH OTHER.

Although I was still clinging to any last hope of swinging Andrea in my direction, I was beginning to come to grips with the fact that it probably wouldn't happen. What we needed to do here, I was finally realizing, was not to change the other person, but to accept each other. My heart felt heavy.

I also realized that she was afraid that if she followed her heart, I would disapprove of *her*, along with her behavior. In spite of my own pain, I was capable of comforting her. We began to discuss the difference between love and approval, between her and her behavior. I loved her, and there was nothing she could ever do to change that. Although I loved her, I didn't always have to love her behavior. Sometimes I just couldn't. I always approved of *her*—of her being, of her very essence— but this time I could not approve of her behavior. We hugged each other a lot during that time. I promised her that we would continue to hold our relationship very close and very dear. Nothing would change between us. We would have a difference of opinion that we would not be able to bring into alignment, and sometimes that's the case with adults in a variety of situations. We always want those closest to us to be like us, but perhaps the deepest and most mature love develops when we accept each other in spite of the differences. That was my heartfelt assurance to her, and I knew she believed me.

The next step was the appointment with our family doctor, who'd been a friend since before Andrea was born. She insisted that I go with her. I guess I was glad she wanted me to be there, but I was confused as to whether my accompaniment to a physician would signal my consent.

By that time, I could see what was going to happen, but there was still a chance that the doctor would be able to influence Andrea in a way I hadn't been able to. She was so objective and professional. She laid out the realities and the warnings to Andrea. I admitted where I stood on the issue but told her that I was there to support my daughter. She comforted me and said that this did not doom Andrea to a life of promiscuity.

Although we gained a little time in all of those proceedings, it was not the ten or twenty years I had originally hoped for. At least now she was fifteen.

As the saga played on, Andrea didn't change, I didn't change, and our relationship became even stronger. Of course, she didn't become promiscuous, and her actions and behaviors have always been thoughtful and responsible. Her self-esteem grew from solid to more solid. Most important, her value system is one I continue to admire. She learned to set firm boundaries, not to cave in to peer pressure, and she has always had a good reputation and the respect of both peers and adults.

Years later, Andrea told me that those discussions we had when she was fourteen and fifteen were some of the most important ones we ever had, and it was *because* of our conversations that she didn't go off the deep end. She said it was because we were able to talk that she learned so much about sex, sexuality, and relationships, that she maintained her principles, and that she continued to live an upright lifestyle. Certainly it involved Brian himself because he was such an upstanding young man who cared about Andrea's well-being and her reputation as much as he cared about his own.

Andrea continued to think those conversations were important as she grew older. She even said she wished her friends had had them with *their* mothers because it would have saved them so much pain and heartache. She also told me she shared those conversations with her next boyfriend who, after many years, has now become her husband.

I understand now that Andrea was not asking my permission to have sex with her boyfriend. She was offering me an invitation to talk about a decision she'd already made. I wanted to have control over her decision, but I did not. We parents just don't have the power we might like to have over our kids. At the time, the only control I had was whether or not I would have input into her life as she made her own decision. If I'd chosen to decline her invitation and forbidden her to have sex, she most likely would have done it anyway, and she would have missed out on my teachings, my experience, and my advice.

It was at this time with Andrea that I began to realize that it's not always what your kids *do* that counts; it's what they learn from it and how they grow and develop into responsible young adults. It's not always the moment that's important, but what happens in the long haul.

Being a parent is not about having everything go as you'd like it to go. Giving counsel is the best we can hope for. We have input, but we don't get to determine the outcomes. Parenthood is about having a relationship in which your kids come to you in times of trouble and need, for counsel and advice, to share the bad as well as the good. During Andrea's decision time, we were there together, side by side.

Drugs: Don't Avoid the Subject

Drugs and alcohol *will* come up for your kids. Neither you nor they can avoid it. When this issue comes up, it is one of the most important times to be the one your kids talk to and listen to most. Sometimes we parents struggle with how to talk with our kids about drugs and alcohol because we don't have enough information, so it's important for us to get some. We also realize that we don't have answers and we don't have solutions. We only have fears that our children will get hooked and fall into the decrepit lifestyle of the drug culture. Thank goodness we don't have to be experts; we only have to be good enough. That means being authentic, open, nonjudgmental, and willing to share our own feelings and experiences.

Many parents shy away from talking with their kids about this complex subject—or they offer just one word of advice: "Don't." The real message that gets conveyed is, "I don't approve, and you're on your own with this one."

Ongoing conversations offer you an enormous opportunity to guide your children and help them through the labyrinth. My advice is this: Talk, communicate, don't worry about whether you express yourself perfectly—just express yourself. Make drugs and alcohol a permitted topic, not a forbidden topic.

> MY ADVICE IS THIS: TALK, COMMUNICATE, DON'T WORRY ABOUT WHETHER YOU EXPRESS YOURSELF PERFECTLY—JUST EXPRESS YOURSELF. MAKE DRUGS AND ALCOHOL A PERMITTED TOPIC, NOT A FORBIDDEN TOPIC.

Several years ago a girlfriend shared with me that she was afraid her teenage daughter was using drugs. She had no evidence and no proof, only a suspicion. When I asked if she'd talked with her daughter about it, she replied, "Oh, no! I'm afraid that if I'm wrong and she's not using, a conversation about it will plant the seed and give her the idea to start."

I was dumbfounded by my friend's naïveté. She believed in waiting until her child was already caught up in drug use before addressing the issue. Isn't it a little late in the game by then? Doesn't it make more sense to get out on the field *before* the other team has scored its first point?

Some parents are afraid of telling their kids about their own drug experiences. I've heard people say, "I could never tell my own kids about my drug and alcohol days. I was so wild and crazy, and I'm just lucky to be alive."

I understand the parents' fear of a child adopting an if-Mom-or-Dad-can-do-it-so-can-I frame of mind. They think it will give kids permission to use. I disagree hugely, because here is the real message: "I'm human. I'm not perfect. I understand something about drugs and the issues you face with friends, in school, and at parties. I've done some things in my life that I'm not proud of, and I want to help you learn from my experience."

I BELIEVE IT'S A MISTAKE *NOT* TO SHARE YOUR PERSONAL EXPERIENCES.

Because this is a powerful statement about your understanding and lack of judgment, I believe it's a mistake *not* to share your personal experiences.

I've also heard parents say, "Well, there isn't much to tell. I really didn't do anything." Whether your experience with drugs has been significant, minimal, or nonexistent is not the point. The point is to share your experiences honestly with your kids so they know drugs and alcohol are not forbidden topics. Don't close that door—or you leave your child alone on the other side of it. If you've never experimented at all, share that, along with your reasons and your experiences of nonuse. Not every parent has a series of trauma-dramas, painful episodes, or wild stories to relate to their kids, but every parent has his or her own story. That's the story you should tell your children. It's all grist for the conversation mill.

I didn't know of any magic bullet that would keep my kids from doing drugs or prevent them from becoming addicted. I believed my best shot at persuading them away from drugs, including cigarettes and alcohol, was embedded in our relationship. I talked with them so that they would know as much about drugs as possible—and from every angle. I believed I could increase the odds of their not using by being able to have a running commentary about drugs. There are three reasons to talk with your kids about drugs:

- If you share, your kids will share
- To teach them what you have learned
- To help them understand addiction and, if needed, heal from their childhood

While I hope your family's experiences with drugs and alcohol were less destructive than ours, these principles hold for any kids. Honest, open conversation about how drugs had an impact or could have an impact on your family is your best hope for helping your kids understand what's dangerous and what's not.

Reason #1: If You Share, Your Kids Will Share

Since drugs and alcohol have permeated my family's history, our story may be longer than most, but I wanted my kids to know their family history and be able to come to me when they needed help making decisions. Therefore, we've been talking about drugs for most of my kids' lives.

The recurring topic for us, of course, was my ex-husband's addiction, which destroyed a chunk of his life, a chunk of mine, and also a big piece of my daughters' lives. I wanted to help them avoid the pitfall of addiction, not only for themselves but also for my future grandchildren, because addiction runs in families. In our family, it was time to turn the ship of addiction around. I was counting on Carol and Andrea from very early on to put their future families on a new and healthier course.

Some people can play with drugs and then walk away, but I always wanted my girls to know that they were at great risk of addiction. Because addiction is in their family, they're more likely than others to be the ones who cannot walk away. I always told them that when the bell sounds and the gates open and the horses run out to begin their race, their two horses are already three-quarters of the way around the track. They have to be very careful because they start with a handicap. They needed to know this, and I would have been remiss if I hadn't told them everything I knew to protect them from making unhealthy choices and ruining their lives.

I wanted to have deep, meaningful conversations with them about the reality of using drugs and drinking excessively. I wanted to scrape past the statistics and the routine warnings, move beyond the "just say no" mentality, and get down to the nitty-gritty. I wanted to be able to bust open the prevailing drug culture's fantasies about the excitement, the curiosity, the lure, and the partying. The teenage drug scene is about being cool; it's about the big high; it's about having fun. It never includes the grit, the crime, the disease, the sorrow, the pain, the date rape, the loss, and the sleaze that the drug world encompasses.

Because of our relationship, I had already earned the right to talk with my daughters forthrightly and blatantly. I already had their ear, so I told Carol and Andrea about my encounters with drugs and people using drugs, not to entertain them, but to educate them, and at the depth that was appropriate and meaningful for their ages. Ultimately, I did this so they'd feel comfortable in talking with me about whatever might happen in their lives.

I wanted to know what they were thinking. I wanted to know their concerns, their questions, and if they were contemplating trying drugs.

I wanted to understand the peer pressure. I wanted to know all these things, so I tried to notice little openings when it would be appropriate to bring up the subject. When Andrea was still young, I had a row of vitamin bottles on a kitchen shelf. She watched me swallow those pills every morning and then asked me one day why I took drugs on a regular basis. She added that she was afraid I'd become addicted like her daddy. It was perfect timing for me not only to answer her questions but also to talk with her about drugs in general.

Kids are usually thinking more than they're saying, so you have to stay attuned to their comments as inroads to their deeper thoughts. Often they test the waters: they sometimes throw out a question to see how you'll react. It's like a thermometer telling them whether they can really trust you, whether they can tell you more. If you're open, listening, and nonjudgmental, it's like a reading of eighty-five degrees: Jump in, the water's fine; let's explore the issue. If you respond curtly, it's like a reading of forty-seven degrees: Stay out, the water's pretty icy; let's *not* talk about the issue. You're either not interested, you're uncomfortable with the topic, or you're sure to be critical. They'll never dive in. It's important to keep the water heated to the perfect conversational temperature.

> KIDS ARE USUALLY THINKING MORE THAN THEY'RE SAYING, SO YOU HAVE TO STAY ATTUNED TO THEIR COMMENTS AS INROADS TO THEIR DEEPER THOUGHTS. OFTEN THEY TEST THE WATERS: THEY SOMETIMES THROW OUT A QUESTION TO SEE HOW YOU'LL REACT.

Reason #2: To Teach Them What You Have Learned

I've watched plenty of people pretend to be having a grand time while hiding behind the fake front of their drugs. They tried to act cool, but underneath they were too uncomfortable with themselves to meet the world straight on and sober. They spent money they couldn't afford. They hung out with people who had no goals beyond getting to the next party and no direction for their lives other than finding enough drugs. They were content to let one day after the other slip away, never to be relived.

For a very brief period in my life, I revealed to my daughters, I'd experimented with a few of these drugs. I explained that I'd walked away from all of that, realizing the party scene was not for me. It never worked for me; I didn't even enjoy it. I'd simply rather be up the next morning, skiing the fresh powder on a sunny blue-sky day, than lying in bed with my head under a pillow, sleeping off a binge from the night before. Not everyone can try drugs and then stop the way I did. I shared with my girls that you can never know in advance if you'll be the one who'll play with the drugs and then walk away when the game is over, or if you'll be the one who becomes addicted. If you become addicted, you have no way of predicting whether you'll be fortunate enough to be the one who can avail yourself of help, or if you'll be the one who'll waste your life in a sewer filled with alcohol or drugs or both, or if you'll be the one who dies. You just can't predict how drugs will affect you or the people you love.

One of the saddest and most shocking phone calls I ever received informed us that my ex-husband's best friend had died of an overdose. He had partied with his friends the night before, just like so many other nights, but that morning he didn't wake up. When they did the autopsy, they found excessive amounts of cocaine and heroin in his blood. It was a dreadfully sad and mournful funeral. He was a great guy, and he was only twenty-five when he unwittingly stuffed too many chemicals into his body. I've often thought, in the thirty or so intervening years, that I've continued to live a full and rich life, and all that time he's been dead simply because he chose to use drugs. I talked with my kids about all of this so they could see how every choice they might make could have a serious impact on them and those who loved them. Both Carol and Andrea have told me that all our early discussions about drugs and alcohol made a huge impact on them and were the determining factor in their decisions not to get involved in drugs even though kids around them were diving in.

Reason #3: To Help Them Understand Addiction and, if Needed, Heal from Their Childhood

Drugs really tore us up. I only knew secondhand how drugs affected my clients and other people in our community, but I know firsthand how my ex-husband's destructive behavior turned all of us upside down. I believed that understanding addiction would help prevent my daughters from becoming addicted themselves.

My ex-husband was a loving, generous, happy-go-lucky young man, but his drug use took him away from us because he needed cocaine more than he needed his family. I've talked with my girls about all of the things that happened—the times when he wasn't there, when he let us down, when he was sick from his drug use, when he embarrassed me, when I embarrassed myself. There are many stories, and my kids have heard them all. Those stories are about heavy drug use and addiction that can disintegrate a family, but the girls hung on, and we made it through. We not only survived, we have thrived—only, I believe, because we finally talked and talked and talked. In the end, it was our relationship and our ability to share with each other that allowed them to begin to heal from the deeply rooted and painful feelings that had piled up inside over all those years.

Today, many more drugs are available than when I was young, and they're more complex, more addictive, and more dangerous than ever before. They're not only more readily available, they're available to younger and younger kids. As parents and stepparents, we have a huge job before us when we begin to deal with drugs with our children. A vital thing to remember is that, even though the drugs are different and more powerful than the ones we know most about, the underlying issues are the same, and the opportunity to influence and guide our children is still available. The key is to stay connected. I've never seen a client in therapy for drug-related issues who had shared openly with their parents when they were young. Bottom line: Talk to your kids about drugs and alcohol.

Different People, Different Stories

Some time ago a young woman in her twenties walked into my therapy office heavily laden with guilt and shame. She was soft-spoken and teary-eyed as she told me she had made an appointment to have an abortion the very next day. At the last minute she'd become confused and frightened and needed someone to talk to. After our session she was still confused and frightened, but at least we had been able to discuss some things she had never thought about before or talked about with anyone. I didn't know what her final decision would be.

About a week later she called me again. She had had the abortion and wanted to talk about the ensuing deep and painful feelings of the whole situation. It was actually her second abortion—the first one had been when she was still a teen. As we dove into her issues, she said she had never talked with her parents about sex or anything related. Her mom had never broached the subject, and my client had never asked any questions. In fact, she couldn't imagine having such a conversation with either of her parents. I was glad to be a person this young woman could finally talk to, although I couldn't help but think that we were ten to fifteen years too late. I also wished the person she had chosen to talk to could have been her mom rather than her therapist.

Another time a family came to see me for therapy—a mom, a dad, and their teenage daughter Jenna. Mom had been a recovering alcoholic for many years, and Dad barely drank out of respect and support for his wife. They had strong morals, good family values, and loved doing things with their kids. But they didn't talk with them about what was going on in their lives in a way that made the kids feel comfortable opening up. Dad was quite opinionated and threw out quick remarks and definitive judgments, cutting off Jenna's ability to engage in dialogue. Mom was quieter and had never learned to express what she thought or felt, so they hardly ever had mother-daughter conversations.

> EVERY FAMILY HAS ITS OWN SET OF VALUES, BUT IT'S IMPORTANT NOT ONLY TO MODEL IT BUT ALSO TO TALK ABOUT IT.

Every family has its own set of values, but it's important not only to model it but also to talk about it. Jenna missed out on the teaching and didn't get the guidance that might have directed her away from drugs. At fifteen she was already smoking pot heavily, so her parents sent her off to a long-term rehabilitation program. When she returned, the family still didn't talk, so Jenna didn't get the support at home to help her stay clean. She found a boyfriend who preferred smoking pot to doing almost anything else. She fumbled through high school, then quit college because her addiction to pot left her too lethargic and unmotivated to study.

It was only then that the parents decided to seek therapy. This was the first time they began to practice *really* talking with each other—listening to one another and exploring the problems. Of course, that was very good for all of them, but unfortunately, Jenna had already wasted several years of her life.

Having grown up with an addicted parent, my own daughters were very afraid of both drugs and alcohol. They decided early on that they would never use either—especially cocaine, their dad's drug of choice. However, the pressures of growing up in today's world, the natural curiosities about drugs and alcohol, and the seemingly innate need kids have to experiment shifted that early decision somewhat. They both tried drinking in high school. In college Carol experimented for a short time with drugs and Andrea tried them once. Today they drink moderately and don't use drugs at all.

Both of them say that their decision to be responsible drinkers and to *not* get involved in drugs was because of all the talking we did when they were children and teenagers. Carol adds, "My decision was very much grounded in the relationship we had as a family. If it hadn't been for our relationship, I could have easily made a different choice."

What's amazing to me is that it seems there's no way for a teen or a young adult to avoid exposure to drugs. They're so pervasive that every kid will most assuredly run into them and be forced to make a decision, on the spot, about whether to use them or not. It's a frightening thought for a parent that when that moment comes, you won't be there to influence or protect your children. All the influence and protection needs to have come *before* that moment. That's why it's time to start talking about drugs now. Don't wait.

Rock 'n' Roll: Media Is All Around Us

If there's any aspect of society that brings to light the need for a strong relationship between parents and children, it's the arena of media and technology. Music and movies, YouTube and MySpace, video games and text messages—it's impossible to keep up. (No doubt, by the time this book is in print, my list will be outdated already.)

Shock radio, soft porn during prime time TV, radical movies intended to offend—all point to the coarsening of popular culture. There seems to be a fascination with the illicit, the perverted, the gory, and the ugly. Perhaps the intrigue has always been there, but as parents, we can't help but wonder if there is any limit at all.

There are no answers to these problems. As individual parents we can't stop the pathway of these trends and can only hope to have minimal influence on their course. We can rarely control what goes on outside our front door, but we certainly have significant impact within our own homes.

If you rely only on policing to keep your children from getting involved where you don't want them to, you will surely lose the battle. This is most definitely the time to stay connected with your kids—talking with them and listening to them—or you'll find yourself in choppy seas, fighting the whitecaps of media and technology on a dark night with no beacon to light your way to safety.

What can you do to protect your child? I have only one piece of advice: Talk constantly with your children; maintain an open and communicative relationship; stay connected. It's the best chance you have to protect them from the rough, raw world media and technology can shove into their lives.

Recently a mom brought her young adolescent to me because he suffered from attention deficit disorder. Josh was a bright kid, but the severity of his ADD made it difficult for him to keep up with his classmates in school, so he was put in special ed classes. He interpreted special ed to mean that he was dumb, he couldn't achieve, and he didn't fit in. He was one of the youngest kids in his class and a late bloomer. Not having developed social skills like the other boys he hung out with, he was often shunned or scorned. Put all of this together and you have a depressed, angry kid who would rather be alone than risk the ridicule of his peers.

Even if adolescent boys were naturally inclined to share feelings, neither Josh nor his parents had the skills to talk about these issues he faced every day. He began to balk at his parents' suggestions to participate in activities with his classmates. He preferred shutting himself in his room and playing video games. He spent four hours a day with his various gaming systems, barely wanting to be interrupted for dinner.

We all know that video games today are complex, popular, and fun—almost addictive. They can cast kids in the roles of baseball players and basketball heroes, but they can also make them carjackers, shooters who gun down police officers, spies, and thugs who commit varieties of other crimes, filling their minds with exciting visuals of violence. Although there's some disagreement about the degree of relationship between virtual violence in video games and actual physical aggression, there's no doubt that the teenage brain is still developing in the prefrontal cortex area, where the impulse control center lies. It's a scary thought that children today are rehearsing violence for hours on end at a time in their lives when their ability to control their own impulses, now influenced by these violent, crime-filled games, has not fully developed.

> IT'S A SCARY THOUGHT THAT CHILDREN TODAY ARE REHEARSING VIOLENCE FOR HOURS ON END AT A TIME IN THEIR LIVES WHEN THEIR ABILITY TO CONTROL THEIR OWN IMPULSES, NOW INFLUENCED BY THESE VIOLENT, CRIME-FILLED GAMES, HAS NOT FULLY DEVELOPED.

In addition, these games disconnect kids from their world and everyone in it. Josh didn't talk to his parents because he was hardly ever with them. They could only surmise what was going on in his life because he only responded to them with sullen grunts and "I dunno." Even though they wanted to help their son with his struggles, they had allowed technology to intervene and disrupt their opportunity to stay connected to him. This would have been a great opportunity for them to fall back to the concepts of rebuilding their relationship with him—doing things with him and spending time just being with him.

Internet Activities

The Internet presents a particularly hard place to protect children, since it is vast, unpoliced, and indispensable to today's kids (and adults, too). The Internet helps kids explore information, learn, and communicate with each other and the world at large. It's also filled with sex, porn, and violence, and the ease with which perverted adults take advantage of naïve and innocent kids is shocking. To help make children safer, parents need to talk with their kids about stranger rules online and discuss Internet activities just as they talk about any other activities their kids are involved in.

Understanding the latest in locking, blocking, and monitoring is certainly helpful, but it's not the sharpest tool in your box. It's not as effective as you might think because you simply can't stay ahead of children whose intent is to get into Web sites you don't want them to get into. You can't watch them every single minute on their computers, their BlackBerrys, their iPhones, or the toys of their friends. In fact, it's impossible for parents—no matter how young, hip, or technologically astute—to guard against kids checking into blogs and chat rooms that are disturbing, disreputable, disgusting, and even dangerous.

THE SHARPEST TOOL YOU POSSESS COMES FROM YOUR RELATIONSHIP WITH YOUR CHILDREN AND YOUR ABILITY TO TALK WITH THEM ABOUT ETHICS, MORALS, AND VALUES.

The sharpest tool you possess comes from your relationship with your children and your ability to talk with them about ethics, morals, and values.

A couple of years ago a mom came to me for therapy. In the course of our conversations she talked about her two preadolescent children, a boy and a girl. They've always talked. Her kids tell her everything, and they enjoy their conversations together. They're very close and connected. Still, she and her husband are concerned about what can seep into their lives from a distorted and perverted world. They've taken measures to help ensure the protection of their kids. They've devoted one room in their house as the computer room. All four of them have their own stations with their four computers lined up around the room. That way, as their mom explained, both parents can easily see what their kids are looking at on their computer screens. It promotes a culture of openness with all of them and continues to keep them connected in a most natural way.

I believe that the best way to influence your own children positively, in order to counteract the negative influences bombarding them from every direction, is to build good, strong relationships with them early on, when they're too young to have any interest at all in media, CDs, computers, the Internet, and video games. Don't underestimate the power of this relationship when those whitecaps begin to crash onto your shores, because it will give you the opportunity to talk with your kids. The trust you've built with them will open the doors for them to share with you, and the connection you've secured with them will allow you to advise and counsel them toward healthy decisions.

Dear Carol and Andrea,

When you were each born, the first thing your dad and I did was to examine every inch of your little bodies. Ahhh! Everything was there and in the right place.

Then the doctor assured us that all your organs functioned as they were intended to, and we felt thrilled and relieved. You were both miracles of perfection. Genetics had done their job. As naïve young parents we assumed that was the most important part. Little did we know that, beyond these physical characteristics, self-esteem would be an even more significant aspect of how you would live out your lives.

Too bad the doctor can't give inoculations against the "germs" that threaten self-esteem. It took me a while to figure out that I was responsible for giving you those injections of wisdom and love—slowly, gradually, over time—by way of talking to you and treating you with respect and by showing you that I believed in you. And I believe in you now as much as I ever have.

I love you bushels and nightgowns,

Mom

CHAPTER 8

Your Potential to Reach for the Stars:

Boosting Your Kids' Self-esteem

WHEN CAROL AND ANDREA WERE YOUNG, I didn't fully understand the importance of believing in yourself, of having a can-do mentality, or of nurturing a positive attitude toward achieving your goals. Only later did it become very clear to me that their self-esteem would be a huge predictor of their success in life. Over the years, I learned the importance of giving my daughters consistent positive messages about themselves. It is an essential part of parenting to bolster your kids' self-esteem as much as possible to give them every opportunity to reach their dreams.

I was reminded of the importance of self-esteem when I went to a memorial service for Maddy Bruger, a woman from our church. When my kids were young, Maddy had spent many holidays with us, and her myriad phone calls would interrupt us at any time of day or night when she was in trouble or felt particularly lonely.

Other than being about the same age and living in the same town, Maddy and I did not have many similarities. She was not nearly as fortunate as I was. Maddy had been born with multiple disabilities: She was legally blind without glasses and legally deaf without a hearing aid. She had a cleft palate and a harelip that had left her with a speech impediment so severe you could barely understand a word she said. She was usually depressed and often suicidal, and she had scarred much of her body, especially her arms, with self-inflicted cuts and burns. It was easy to recognize Maddy walking down the street because she was always trudging along, head downcast, dressed in the oddest assortment of layered clothing, carrying multiple plastic bags.

Way back when my children were babies, a group of women in the church recruited me to join them in trying to help Maddy. It was a daunting thought because none of us really understood who Maddy was. She was an enigma, a most eccentric young woman living in an unbearable physical and emotional pain we knew little about. We also believed that, without our help, she would surely kill herself. We took turns inviting her to join our families for Thanksgiving, Christmas, and Easter. We never missed throwing birthday parties for her, even though her special day landed on the same day as Carol's. We alternated weeks to call her and take her out for lunch. If we ever forgot, she let us know, in no uncertain terms, that we had abandoned her and left her to fend for herself. We bought her gifts, gave her food and clothing, and visited her at her apartment, which she kept in hovel style, always so cluttered you could hardly find a spot to sit down. Over the years, we painted her walls, cleaned out her junk, drove her to appointments, and checked on her when she was absent from a church event. Her phone calls could easily last an hour. She called to complain, to emote, or to chat when she was lonely, angry, suicidal, and occasionally even feeling good. I got to the point where I could decipher her unintelligible speech patterns and follow her conversations.

My little group was not the only one. Employers in town offered her menial jobs so she'd have some cash and a purpose to her days. Doctors and dentists saw her free of charge. A local psychologist saw her gratis for more than twenty-six years, every Wednesday at twelve-thirty. He was a saint and certainly one of the most important people in Maddy's life. She would never have made it without him and the church, her second home and her refuge. A veritable cadre of people surrounded Maddy's life to her very last day. I'm relieved to know that she passed away peacefully and of natural causes. I'm also confident that every single person who came to her side felt blessed by Maddy's presence in our lives because she stretched us in becoming more tolerant, less judgmental, more compassionate, and more appreciative of our own lives.

You may still be wondering what was the root cause of Maddy's catastrophic life. Most of us learned only bits and pieces along the way. We never knew anything about her mother, but we gradually found out that she had suffered terrible post-traumatic stress from having been abused physically, psychologically, and sexually by her father and older brother. They didn't just molest her. They tortured her in unimaginable ways, and they did it from the day she was born until she was old enough to leave home. Whenever she was inside their house, she was at risk, so she learned to stay outside for hours, playing with animals. As you might surmise, animals became her best friends, the only living beings she could trust not to hurt her. That explains why, as an adult, her dogs were always so vitally important to her. She learned to fantasize because it was a way to escape the memories of her horrendous reality. Sometimes she could lose track of reality for six months at a time, which now makes me realize why it seemed as if she was constantly lying and telling stories that made no sense.

Maddy lived a tormented life, not so much because of the cards that genetics had dealt her, but because of the way she'd been treated by her significant caregivers. Instead of helping and nurturing her, those caretakers treated her inhumanely. Rather than bolstering her self-esteem and instilling in her a belief that she could overcome her physical difficulties, they ripped and shredded and mangled her self-esteem to such a degree that she tried to destroy herself over and over. Although her father and brother had died many years before, she was never rid of them. The emotional and psychological damage they had inflicted on her lived on within her for the rest of her days. Thanks to them, she lived out her entire life in survival mode, never even glimpsing an inkling of what it might feel like to thrive.

Maddy was an intelligent, quick-witted woman who was skilled in a variety of crafts, but her father and brother had brutally hacked off so many pieces of her world, she could not rise up and take charge of her life. Yet she was tough. She never lost her deep and abiding faith in God, she continued to reach out to people, she gave what she could, and she helped others in the best way she knew how. I can only wonder what her life might have been like if her father had given her a chance.

WE SOMETIMES SAY THAT THE GOAL OF ADULTHOOD IS TO RECOVER FROM CHILDHOOD.

In the psychological world, we sometimes say that the goal of adulthood is to recover from childhood. That's a potent admission to the influence of parents on their children. In Maddy's case, she was never able to recover because, on a scale from minus ten to plus ten, she had too far to go, just to get out of the negative. She started at such a disadvantage because the most significant people in her life had beaten her down when she was too small to know there was anything else in life and too young to be able to fight back. It drives home the point that it is incumbent upon all parents, and even all adults, to build up children, whether they are your own or someone else's, and to never tear them down.

They Gotta Believe

In the past few years, Lou Tice has become a household name in our family because his books, seminars, and CDs have contributed so much to my understanding of self-esteem and how we can achieve our potential. It was from Lou Tice that I began to understand more fully that children will succeed, not at the level of their capacity but rather at the level they *believe* in their capacity. This is an important concept for parents to understand, because if kids were truly to perform at their real level of ability, then our job would be much easier. We could sit back, relax, and watch them grow and develop without thinking too much about our participation. The pressure would be off. Unfortunately, that's not the case. Since our children will perform based on how they *believe* they can perform, we have the ongoing responsibility and exciting opportunity to help them shape that belief in themselves.

The day each of my daughters entered the world, part of their lives was already carved in granite. Their genes would establish certain unalterable parameters. But much of them hadn't even begun to develop. Their attitudes and perceptions of the world, their spirit and tenderness of heart, their feelings and beliefs about themselves were yet to be etched into their minds. How each of those things grew and evolved would determine their self-esteem and their journey through life. It was only in hindsight that I realized how much I had to do with all of that. Carol and Andrea have always been the actors in their own play, but their dad and I decorated the set, created the lighting, designed the costumes, and even wrote large chunks of the script. Though we didn't know it at the time, we were hugely influential in how they acted out their roles.

Parents and stepparents need to realize the enormity of our impact on our kids. When Carol and Andrea were both young, they listened to my words, watched my facial expressions, and heard my tone of

PARENTS AND STEPPARENTS NEED TO REALIZE THE ENORMITY OF OUR IMPACT ON OUR KIDS.

voice. They could tell instantly whether I spoke to them approvingly or with disappointment. Even though their brains were not developed enough to think abstractly or reason wisely, their emotional systems were complete, and they constantly absorbed a wide range of feelings. They may not have been able to name those feelings, but they bore into the girls' minds with the power of an indelible stamp. My interactions with them blasted their way into their psyches and left an imprint on their burgeoning self-esteem. When I treated them with respect, honoring who they were as people, it was like blowing up each girl's self-esteem balloon as big and light and expansive as it could get. If I'd treated them with disregard—ignoring them, scorning them, putting them down, or, God forbid, abusing them—it would have been like puncturing their self-esteem balloons until they were lying flat in the dirt. Although I realize I was only one piece of the puzzle, I was, nonetheless, a big piece. Not only did I have the inherent power to make them feel good or bad in the moment, but over time the messages I gave them on a daily basis began to formulate the self-esteem they would carry with them for the rest of their lives.

Children don't develop self-esteem in a vacuum or just at home. As my girls grew older, a lot of people contributed to how they felt about themselves. Children's self-esteem comes first from the significant people around them, even before they can internalize it and make it their own. My daughters were lucky that most of those people—other family members, friends, teachers, coaches, and camp counselors, to name a few—were positive influences on them and let them know that they were capable young women.

That wasn't true of everyone all the time. As a parent, I found it nearly impossible for me to always keep my daughters out of harm's way. I simply couldn't control what other people did or said, but I could always control myself. I tried to utilize our relationship to talk with them about what was happening daily. That way, I could keep abreast of how things were going for them on a personal level. By constantly giving them positive messages, I hoped to counteract any negatives they got from anyone else. A lot of people influenced how they felt about themselves, but none of them more dramatically than their father and me.

It was an awesome and humbling realization that I had the power to instill in my daughters a strong, broad, and unencumbered belief in their own potential—or I could cripple them. Simply by giving them can't-do messages, such as "you're stupid," "you're incompetent," or "I don't like who you are," I would have shrunk the possibilities for their lives. The gradual understanding of this concept created within me an enormous sense of responsibility to treat them in such a way that they could maximize their positive beliefs in themselves. I wanted to set the bar high for each of them, not in the sense of creating pressure for them to do what I wanted or what was beyond their abilities or desires, but in the sense of lifting the lid off of their limitations, supporting them in dreaming big dreams, and encouraging them to reach toward their goals and dreams without restrictions. I tried to make our relationship reflect my belief in them because I believed it fell to me, first and foremost, to help them be the very best they could be. To do otherwise would have been to abrogate my responsibility as their mom. It's an incredible opportunity that many parents don't understand, and it's much more exciting than most parents think.

I believe that parents can help kids adopt three ideas that create self-esteem:

- A can-do mentality
- A sense of deserving
- A feeling of empowerment

Each of these aspects can be developed individually. But in combination, they can show your kids their own potential—and then there's no stopping them!

Self-esteem Idea #1:
A Can-do Mentality

A can-do mentality means an attitude that you can face what's coming and achieve what you reach for, and parents can support it simply by acting as though they, too, believe that their kids will accomplish whatever they set out to do. My dad was a terrific model of the can-do mentality for me. He was raised in a small farming community in the Midwest, one of the youngest of eleven siblings. They were poor, and Dad worked hard to help support his very large family. He used to tell me about how his father, my grandfather, ridiculed him and laughed at him when he spoke of his goals for accomplishing things in his own life. Dad vowed he would never do that to his own children, so when I was growing up, he made a special effort to tell me, my brother, and my two sisters how great we were. The four of us chuckle even today at his consistent descriptor. According to him, we were all "outstanding."

Repeatedly, he would say, "Just ask anyone—the teachers, the banker, the Sunday school teachers—they will all say you are outstanding." He was doing the best he could to boost our self-esteem and make us believe we could do anything we wanted to.

That one little word has been a powerhouse for me. Long ago, it embedded itself deep within my brain, where it took root and grew. Throughout my life, whenever my confidence flailed or my doubts flooded over me, I could pull out that precious word, along with the surrounding strong feeling of my dad's belief in me, and march on.

Just as my dad's words have stuck with me, so will mine stick with my daughters. The messages, both verbal and nonverbal, that I gave them when they were growing up have become engraved in their minds and their spirits, and those messages will continue to live on inside them even after I am gone.

> THE MESSAGES, BOTH VERBAL AND NONVERBAL, THAT I GAVE THEM WHEN THEY WERE GROWING UP HAVE BECOME ENGRAVED IN THEIR MINDS AND THEIR SPIRITS, AND THOSE MESSAGES WILL CONTINUE TO LIVE ON INSIDE THEM EVEN AFTER I AM GONE.

Long ago when I first got the idea that I wanted to have a close relationship with Carol and Andrea, I had no idea what it really meant. Even when they were very young, I already loved who they were, so it was natural to want to be close to them. Back then I thought the main benefit of our relationship would be that we could be friends, that we could enjoy hanging out together, and that, when they needed help or advice, I'd be the first person they sought out. Indeed, all of that did happen, and the friendships we have are the dearest and most precious ones in my life. Now I understand much better that the other benefit of our relationship, the more important benefit, was to be able to impact their self-esteem in a positive way. The wish and prayer of every parent for their child should be this: *I hope I have done my job well enough so that you can allow your self-esteem to soar and act upon your potential to reach for the stars.*

Self-esteem Idea #2: A Sense of Deserving

A sense of deserving means a belief that we are worthy of good things. Not entitled in that the world owes us, in that we can do no wrong, in that everything should naturally revolve around us. That's not what I mean. In fact, I'd call that grandiosity. It's selfish and self-centered to the max—even narcissistic. No, I mean deserving of happiness, of a loving relationship, of a healthy self-esteem. We want to teach our children to feel deserving of good things. Not because they're special, but simply because they exist.

Sadly, Terry confesses that he got the message from his father that he really wasn't deserving of anything too extravagant. Terry began to believe that squeaking by should be good enough. Asking for his share, requiring to be treated fairly, expecting to get what he paid for—all of these were beyond his reach. In some respects he learned to settle for what came his way and be grateful. I was fortunate to be able to get to know his dad quite well before he died, and I can say with certainty that he was a gentle, loving man who delighted in the successes of his three sons. I know he always wanted Terry to have the best life had to offer, but Terry didn't get that message. We'll never know what he really wanted to teach Terry, but somehow, an important lesson—the one that says we deserve—was glossed over.

Terry has always fought for me or for my kids to get what he thought we deserved, but he has rarely stood up for himself. In many ways he has always exuded self-esteem, but in the area of feeling as though *he* deserved, he was deficit. Over time, he came to realize the destructiveness of that undeserving message and has turned it around in his life into one that is much more positive and uplifting. His ongoing regret is that he did not teach a message of deserving to his own three sons because at that time he didn't have it himself, and it's hard work reversing it as an adult.

Like Terry, Carol used to have a hard time standing up for herself or asserting herself confidently. When she was a child, whenever an opportunity came along, she hesitated and allowed another kid to grab the opportunity being offered to her. It was as though she didn't feel she deserved to have it, so she stepped aside and then felt bad when someone else got what she wanted and deserved. I gave a lot of attention to this issue for her because it troubled me deeply. I used to say to her, "Carol, if all the kids in your class were to line up in a row for a reward and the teacher asked each of you to take one step, which direction would you step—forward or backward?"

As we talked about the metaphor, Carol realized that most of her classmates would leap forward to snatch the reward in front of them. Even if there was one reward for each kid, she would be likely to step backward. She was inclined to take the backseat, the crumbs, so as not to seem greedy or selfish. Being gentle, nice, and good-hearted are beautiful attributes, but getting overlooked and stepped on because you don't take care of yourself is another thing altogether.

We continued to work on this issue together as Carol matured, and she has now developed a healthy sense of deserving that has augmented her self-esteem. When I recently asked her how she overcame her inclination to put herself in the background, she said, "I know I did the work myself, but you were always there for me. We just kept talking about it and you kept supporting me. And we celebrated my victories. Whenever I stood up for myself, you asked me what I had done differently and how I felt about it. That helped a lot in giving me little insights into how I could continue to change."

A sense of deserving is an important part of success and self-esteem. It's often what drives you to try harder, to put yourself out beyond your ordinary limits, to reach for your goal even though it seems to be dancing far away from you. Success doesn't just come swimming into your arms. You have to make things happen for yourself, whether it's a loving relationship or a dynamite career. No one

A SENSE OF DESERVING IS AN IMPORTANT PART OF SUCCESS AND SELF-ESTEEM.

can make it happen for you. Down underneath, if you don't believe you deserve, you will surely sabotage your own efforts to get ahead.

In my therapy practice, I've worked with many clients who haven't felt as though they deserved, and the message almost always stems from childhood. When we're adults, it takes a lot of work to reverse that message. We parents have the opportunity to shortcut the process if we are alert. We can begin to talk with our kids early on to help them do what Carol did—bust out; believe in herself; and become a person whose competence, character, and skills shine through.

Self-esteem Idea #3:
A Feeling of Empowerment

Empowerment means a sense of being in charge of your own destiny. It's the opposite of being a pawn in a game or a baby to be cared for. This threat to kids' self-esteem is sneaky, because good parents often can run roughshod over kids' empowerment, without having a clue what they're doing.

For instance, my dad was a bit of a control freak. Every time I walked out the door for a Friday night high school football game, he'd lecture me about dressing warmly. He had a dozen strong, unalterable reasons for me to wear a scarf, a hat, and gloves, but the dorky boots to keep my feet from freezing were over the top. He absolutely would not allow me to decide for myself. He loved me unconditionally and wanted the very best for me, but the best was often his way only. I remember those lectures, not because I learned to be wise or to take care of myself, but because he wouldn't let me think for myself. Instead of teaching me to become self-reliant and confident, building my self-esteem, he taught me how controlling and stubborn he could be.

I know how hard it is *not* to control kids. When Carol and Andrea were young, I wanted to tell them what to do, who to be friends with, how to study, when to say yes or no, what to think, how to act, when to go, when to stop, and how high to jump. All because I loved them and thought that telling them everything would save them time, prevent disasters, and smooth out their path. I also had an inkling that, by doing so, I would be doing them a disservice. I knew they had to make their own mistakes, figure out the error of their ways, fall down, and learn to get up on their own. I even remember Carol saying to me once, "I know you're right, Mom, but I just have to do it my own way."

It's a painful process for a parent to watch children flounder and grope to find their way, but you have to let go of them so they can feel empowered to make it on their own. There are a million ways parents can assert control and disempower their kids. Let me tell you about Brad, who was ruled with a heavy, hostile hand. He was only seventeen, a dozen years ago, when he called me to make his first appointment. Hearing his young voice on the phone, I presumed he was in a lot of emotional pain because, in all my years of practicing therapy, I had seen just a handful of teenage boys. Young males usually don't want therapy. Within a short time in my office, Brad made it quite clear that my presumption had been right. He slouched on my sofa and focused his eyes on the rug at his feet as he began to talk. At first he spoke quietly and hesitatingly, as if he were uncomfortable about pouring out his story to a stranger, yet he seemed eager to have someone listen. His father had died when he was young, and he had been raised, an only child, by his mother, who had struggled to make ends meet. As I asked him questions, I learned that she had given him as much love and attention as she had energy for, and he thrived as a bright, confident, social child.

> **IT'S A PAINFUL PROCESS FOR A PARENT TO WATCH CHILDREN FLOUNDER AND GROPE TO FIND THEIR WAY, BUT YOU HAVE TO LET GO OF THEM SO THEY CAN FEEL EMPOWERED TO MAKE IT ON THEIR OWN.**

Brad gained momentum as he continued his story, glancing up at me from time to time to check out the expression on my face and my level of interest in his tale. When he was fifteen, his mother married a man with plenty of money. Perhaps the marriage solved her problems, but it created new ones for Brad. His stepdad, Stuart, was authoritative and controlling. Because Stuart's own kids were grown and gone, Brad felt immediately that he was in the way and not wanted. Brad described his stepdad as acting superior, a guy who knew everything, which made Brad feel as if his own knowledge was inferior or worthless. Stuart often made snide remarks, putting Brad down, like it was a game and he wanted to see how bad he could make Brad feel about himself.

In subsequent sessions Brad described what it felt like to grovel and plead every time he wanted to borrow the car, go to a party, or spend the night with a friend. Often Stuart would yell at him, slinging condescending comments his way, wielding his power over Brad as a lord over his lowly serf. Sometimes Stuart threatened to kick Brad out of the house, or punish him unreasonably if he didn't do as Stuart said. Brad felt diminished, powerless, helpless, and hopeless. What hurt even more was that his mother often stood by, looking helpless herself but not intervening in the heavy control being wielded over her son. Brad felt betrayed by his mom and cruelly ruled by his stepdad. Stuart's control was ruining not only Brad's self-esteem but also his relationship with his mother.

One of the great things about working with young people is that they're often quite open, not hiding anything or holding back. This was certainly true of Brad. He grinned almost sardonically when he told me that he'd finally begun to rebel by sneaking out of the house, taking the car without asking, and adopting a belligerent attitude. Those behaviors had landed him in therapy. When I asked him why he'd started behaving so differently, he said it was the only thing he could think of to get back at his stepdad. Yet Brad felt confused and guilty, not really wanting to hurt his mother.

Although his parents had mandated that he come to see me, Brad was secretly glad to be able to tell someone about his awful situation.

The saddest part of Brad's story, for me, was how he had changed internally within a couple of years. An articulate, mature young man, Brad said he once believed he could do anything he wanted. Now he doubted himself, thinking he had no skills or talents of any value. He used to dream big dreams for his future, but now he rarely dreamed at all, believing he could never achieve what he envisioned. His stepfather's harsh control had shredded his hope for success and pummeled his self-esteem. In therapy we worked on restoring his dreams and creating a new vision for who he wanted to be, where he wanted to go, and what he wanted to do in his life. It was tough work because tearing down someone's self-esteem is easier than building it back up.

Another client's parents disempowered in a totally different way. They used the light, loving touch of control. At sixteen, Sasha came to therapy for an eating disorder. She'd dropped from 125 to 72 pounds within a few months. Her anorexia was so serious that she'd ended up at a treatment center. There, they monitored her eating behaviors and helped her learn to eat healthily again. At the same time, they provided intense psychological therapy. Sasha and I talked quite a bit in my office before she went off to treatment, and what I learned about her confirmed what I had read in the literature about eating disorders.

Sasha's parents were loving, caring, and involved—all the things Sasha could hope for. Except that they exerted a very strong, subtle pressure for her to live her life their way, leaving her own desires and passions squashed. From telling her what extracurriculars she should get involved with, to pressuring her to be friends with certain kids in school, to talking with her about what career they envisioned her having, that subtle control basically said: "We need to do it for you because we don't believe you can do it for yourself."

By the time Sasha became a teenager, she didn't feel very good about herself. She had absorbed the message her parents unintentionally pounded into her—that she was unable to think for herself or take care of herself. The message inside her rang loud and clear: "If you don't comply with my wishes, you'll destroy my expectations of you; you'll disappoint me; I'll feel betrayed." That message had gradually ground down Sasha's self-esteem into bits and pieces. A part of her still wanted to get out from under her parents' control, but she didn't know how.

Sasha was a good girl who didn't have an openly rebellious bone in her body, so she rebelled quietly, at the same level as her parents' pressure, counterbalancing their control over her. She simply chose not to eat. They could control a lot, but they couldn't control what she put into her mouth. Before therapy, she wasn't consciously aware of her rebellion, but she *was* aware of the control pressed upon her under the guise of her parents wanting the best for her.

When Terry and I were visiting once with an old friend who had come to ski for a few days, we began, as always, to catch up by telling each other about our kids. During this visit, our friend was more open than usual as he related some difficulties his adult son was experiencing. Our friend was sorry and saddened to watch his son make career and relationship decisions that were not in his own best interests. Our friend feared his son didn't believe himself able to "go for the gold," and he was, therefore, settling for less than he should. Our friend became introspective over a glass of wine at dinner. He said, "I never really understood until now how important good self-esteem is in making it in the world. My son is intelligent, well educated, and conscientious. He's very capable, but I don't think he knows it. It's so hard to sit back and watch him take what comes to him instead of going for what he wants."

As we talked, our friend got tears in his eyes. He shared that he was just beginning to realize his part in his son's lack of self-esteem. He had always exerted a lot of pressure on his son to do things his way, and that extra pressure made up the difference between guidance and control. Rather than developing an attitude that he could take charge of his life, the son learned to sit back and wait. His dad's control—even though it was well intended—left a big chink in his ability to succeed as an adult.

When I was studying the Myers-Briggs Type Indicator, an instrument to measure personality type, I came across an important teaching of Carl Jung. He believed that our job as parents is to find out who our children really are and then spend the rest of their lives celebrating them. This involves helping them to flourish within the framework of who they are, rather than trying to pack them into the mold we might prefer for them. This is what it means to empower your kids. Whether control is heavy-handed and hostile, or loving and caring, it's disempowering. Control discourages creativity and prevents healthy self-esteem. It also destroys relationships.

> OUR JOB AS PARENTS IS TO FIND OUT WHO OUR CHILDREN REALLY ARE AND THEN SPEND THE REST OF THEIR LIVES CELEBRATING THEM.

Parenting as an Equal

When Carol and Andrea still lived at home, I wanted to minimize the power differential between us rather than to maximize it. I wanted to put us on a more even playing field and create more equality between us. I didn't understand equality to mean that we were the same; rather, it meant that we had equal rights to dignity and respect and that their feelings were equally as important as mine. I figured that if I treated them disrespectfully and as if they were inferior to me, they would grow up to believe they were lower than or less than other people. On the other hand, if I gave them as much power over their own lives as I could, treating them with equality and showing them respect as fellow human beings, it would make them stand tall and believe that they could conquer the world.

Disempowerment feels like your life and your future lie in the hands of someone else. Empowerment feels like you control your own destiny. When Carol went off to college, I think she was ready to grab her next level of empowerment and take charge of her own life. She told me later that she was tired of being a "good girl" and wanted to experiment in partying and being not quite so responsible. She was trying to find herself apart from her identity as a member of our family. She was afraid I would disapprove and judge her, so she became just a little less open with me. Instead of telling me everything, she gave me the tip of the iceberg. Even though I tried to be supportive of her independence, it was difficult not to give controlling advice when she announced that she was going out partying the night before a midterm. I knew I could not control her from a thousand miles away, but I didn't want her to flunk out of school in her quest for her new identity. *I tried to remember that my goal was not to be a perfect mom or to have a perfect daughter.* My goal was to maintain a positive relationship with her, so that when she needed or wanted my advice, she would feel free to talk with me. I held my breath a lot during her first year of college.

One of the cutest things Carol ever said to me was, "Mom, I wish I'd hurry up and get past this stage I'm going through because I miss our old relationship. I miss being close to you." That's when I knew she'd be okay. Since empowerment and self-esteem fit together like a hand in a glove, I was sure that she'd come out on top—and I was right.

The space in between, while our kids are learning to become independent, can be really tough on a parent. That's when you're especially glad you had a strong relationship with them when they were younger that gave you input into their lives. That's also when you're glad you *still* have a close connection with them, so that when they're spreading their wings, they can still reach out to you in their time of need.

Make-believe

When Carol and Andrea were about ten and twelve, they were having one of their sibling squabbles and came to me to set things straight. Since I didn't have a clue how to solve their problem, I flashed upon a plan to include them in the process. I was pleased that my spur-of-the-moment idea not only resolved the issue between them but also made them both feel that they had a lot of personal power.

After they each spilled out their complaints about the other, I suggested that we all three sit cross-legged in a little circle on the floor. They had no idea what was about to happen. Actually, neither did I—I was stalling for time to think. Then I asked each of us to pretend we were one of the other two. I became Andrea, Andrea popped into the character of Carol, and Carol was suddenly Mom. With our new identities, we restated the issues underlying the quarrel and then discussed the resolution from the perspective of the person we had just turned into. It was both hilarious and enlightening. We howled with laughter as each of us, in turn, took on our pretend personality, tone of voice, mannerisms, and point of view. We ended up with a much-better resolution than I could have come up with on my own. Most important, instead of giving all the power to me, they realized they had the tools they needed to solve the conflict themselves. I believe that simple exercise allowed them to grow bigger in their sense of healthy personal power and the feeling that they had the capacity, the intelligence, and the wisdom to solve problems.

The question for every parent is this: Will you be on the lookout for opportunities to make your kids feel good about themselves—to empower them and make them believe in themselves? Or will you tell them what to do and try to solve all their problems for them? You can either *build* their self-esteem or *limit* their self-esteem. The choice is yours.

Just a Little Respect

At the bottom of a good relationship, down deep where the roots grow, lies an essential element for creating real contact with your kids. That ingredient is respect. When Carol and Andrea were children, I believed my respect for them would grow their self-esteem and create a tighter bond in the relationship between us. At the time, I had no idea how much it would mean to me to be respected by them in return.

It was never difficult for me to show my daughters respect when they were growing up. I always liked them. I admired them. I held them in high regard. In fact, it made me angry when other people didn't show them the respect I thought they deserved. I remember dropping the two of them off at the video store to pick up a movie we wanted to watch that evening. I waited and waited for them in the car at the curb, getting impatient at how long they were inside. When they finally emerged, video in hand, I asked them what in the world had taken so much time. They replied that they were standing politely at the counter, ready to pay for our movie, but the clerk kept looking over them to wait on the adult customers behind them. He had ignored them because they were children. I immediately jumped up onto my high horse and raged for a couple of minutes about how disrespectful people were to bypass kids. How could adults think kids would grow up with good self-esteem if the adults disregarded them when they were young? How could kids feel good about themselves if adults dealt with them as lesser human beings? Furthermore, why would adults ever expect to be regarded respectfully by young people if they didn't regard young people with respect?

It was my theory that, if I treated my daughters with respect, then I could expect them to treat me the same way. However, I remember that when Andrea was about eleven years old, she began to go through a phase when it was cool to snicker and roll her eyes at me as if I were the dumbest gourd in town. The first time, it was only a small, snide remark. I jolted a bit, wondering if I'd actually heard it right. Maybe I hadn't understood what she'd said. A couple of days later another remark slid out. The words themselves weren't so ugly, but her tone of voice was belittling and snotty. Again, maybe I didn't get it right. This went on for two or three more weeks. Then one day I was doing my routine chauffeur shift, with Andrea and her friend in the backseat. The two of them began to giggle and whisper. I could see through the rearview mirror that they were looking and pointing at me.

This may sound silly to you, but it hurt my feelings. I began to think about a friend of mine whose teenage daughter had developed a pattern of ridiculing and cutting down her mom in front of others. It made me terribly uncomfortable when the teenage girl did so in front of me, and I vowed that I would never have a child who would intentionally humiliate or insult me in public.

I waited until Andrea's friend went home, and then I sat her down for a little talk. I told her that I had begun to notice a difference in her behavior toward me, and I told her how it made me feel. It made me feel sad, hurt, and disrespected. I didn't tell her that what she had done was wrong. I simply told her how it made me feel. I had waited until it had happened several times before I brought it up, but that day was the first time she had engaged a friend in her new tactics, so it seemed like the appropriate time to address the issue. I also said I was disappointed because I had always hoped we would never stoop to treating each other disrespectfully. Her response indicated she was somewhat confused, as though she didn't really understand what she might have been doing differently. I told her that I would signal her with a code the next time she acted toward me in that hurtful way. I didn't want to embarrass her in front of a friend. Her job would be to figure out what she had done. Bottom line was that I treated her with respect, and I expected the same from her in return. Over the next couple of weeks, I signaled her several times. She obviously took my signaling to heart because that was the end of her disrespectful phase.

The lesson is this: Every time you treat people with disrespect, it makes them feel bad. It doesn't matter whether it's your parent or your child, a teacher or a colleague, an employee or a friend. They may not remember the words you said, but they'll remember how they felt when you said them. Treating others with disrespect has a negative impact on their self-esteem, which is a serious thing for any human being. Even if it's on a subconscious level, their interactions with

> THEY MAY NOT REMEMBER THE WORDS YOU SAID, BUT THEY'LL REMEMBER HOW THEY FELT WHEN YOU SAID THEM.

you, from then on, will be modified by your disrespectful behavior toward them. No one feels good when he or she is treated poorly. No one. Not the waitress, the physician, the bank teller, or the ordinary guy on the street. Not only is it unkind, it's never in your best interest. If you want to be spit on, then spit on someone first. If you want to be hugged, then learn to hug. If you want to be respected in your life, then give respect to others. It will enhance your self-esteem every time.

In relationships, respect is a useless concept unless it is mutual. I would have no reason to think my kids should continue to revere me as their mother if I didn't esteem and honor them as my daughters. When I do, it certainly bolsters their self-esteem. Andrea recently reminded me of an incident with an English teacher when she was in middle school. Her teacher suddenly began to assign 50 vocabulary words for memorization every week. He passed out a new list of words every Friday and told the students to look up the definitions and write each word in a sentence. A selection of those words would be included in their regular weekly test. During the week there was no mention of these words, nor did they work with them in any way in class. By the end of the semester Andrea and her classmates would have been given several hundred vocabulary words. I watched Andrea struggle to memorize these lists for about three weeks. I also watched her promptly forget them the following week. She was a conscientious, straight-A student, and it frustrated me to see her kill herself over a futile memorization effort, so we talked. Then I did something I'd never done before.

I went to the school and made an appointment to see Andrea's teacher. I told him that, although Andrea was trying to carry out his assignment, I'd given her my permission to slack off. I said that, although I believed in developing a large vocabulary, this particular technique was ineffective for her. Andrea and I had decided that rather than 50 words each week, she would pick 10 from his list and commit to using them with me at home all week long in an effort to really learn them. Since she would be learning only 10 new words rather than 50, he could expect that she'd fail the vocabulary section of the test each week. In spite of that, it would be my hope that, by the end of the semester, rather than having wasted many hours memorizing and subsequently forgetting 800 words, she would have integrated 160 new words into her working vocabulary.

As we talked about this incident recently, Andrea reiterated how much she appreciated my going to bat for her. She told me that she felt very respected by me, which bumped her up another notch on her ladder of self-esteem.

Now the tables are beginning to turn, and I feel the mutual respect we have had for each other work in my favor as well. I feel my two daughters starting to parent me in small ways, as I have parented them all these years, but never with resentment, ridicule, or degrading comments. Quite the opposite. The reverence and regard they bestow upon me as I am growing older touches my heart deeply because I know that I really matter to them. They value me as I have always valued them, which means more to me than I know how to express.

Carol and Andrea are both faster and stronger than I am. They learn things more quickly and remember them better. I train for weeks to hike over the mountain, but they come in for the weekend and leave me in the dust. I used to hold each of them by the waist with their skis between mine as we slowly maneuvered down the hill. Now they slow down and coax me to follow them down the really steep and deep runs. They answer my computer questions, they fix my digital camera, they program my iPod. They help me find good airline prices online.

> THEY LIFT ME UP, CONVINCE ME I CAN STILL DO ANYTHING I WANT, AND TELL ME HOW GREAT I AM.

They drive the car while I sit comfortably beside them. They never make me feel old or slow or useless. In fact, they lift me up, convince me I can still do anything I want, and tell me how great I am. Today we have as much fun together as ever.

It's clear to me that a parent's job is never done. Even though my friends and I groan in mutual fatigue from time to time, we wouldn't have it any other way. Parenthood is a lifetime career. No matter how old my daughters get, I will always be concerned for them. I will add their spouses and my grandchildren to my worry list. I will always do my best to encourage them, support them, and help them reach their goals. I will continue, for as long as I am able, to sustain our strong relationship by communicating openly with them, sharing feelings with them, and making them and their families feel a sense of belonging in our family. I hope we will continue to be honest and transparent with each other so that there are never forbidden topics that we can't discuss. Most of all, I want to do everything I know how to do and can do to respect them and make them feel good about who they are.

Self-esteem is a fragile thing. It goes up and down with the winds of life. I hope that my continuing love and support for my children will help keep their winds blowing toward their back, moving them forward. I now understand, more than I ever have before, the expression my father used to say to me: "I would crawl through a sewer for you."

Not only is our parenting job never over, but we parents can start again, wherever we are, and make repairs to the damage caused by our mistakes in the past. Most kids never really give up wanting to have a good relationship with their parents, and they are more willing to forgive than a parent might think. Just a short apology by a parent goes a long way toward mending a broken relationship. I truly believe it's never too late to start, no matter how old the parent or the child. Even in a small way, even if you don't know how, even if you feel you're blundering and stumbling toward your children. It's the movement, the direction, and the intention that count more than the destination.

Adults who have never gotten along well with their parents can begin the process of renewal themselves. I don't know a parent who wouldn't like to have a great relationship with his or her kids—at any age. Sometimes parents get stuck in their own patterns and don't know how to get out, but deep inside, their hearts are always turned toward their children. The ideas and concepts of building relationships work in both directions—from parent to child and also from adult child to parent. It's never too late to start making inroads toward closer connections with those we love.

Several years ago a friend shared with Terry and me that he'd never had a good relationship with his dad and that they'd never hugged. One day he decided that it was simply not okay with him any longer. During the next visit he told his father that he wanted to develop something more between them. He began to talk a little more personally to his dad and ended his visit with a hug. At first his father didn't have much to say, and he hung wooden and uncomfortable in his son's arms, but our friend persisted. Gradually, over time, his father began to open up a bit, and they began to exchange warm, embracing hugs—something that was most fulfilling for our friend. Terry and I both believe that his dad had always wanted what our friend began to create between them. He just had no idea how to get there by himself.

Parents and their children: these relationships are some of the most complicated that exist. Like most parents, I didn't have it figured out when my daughters were young. But as they became adults, I realized that I had at least reached the first of my original two goals with them: the satisfaction and pleasure of a deep, intimate friendship. I've given them my heart, and I've received from each of them what no other relationship on earth had the potential to give to me. As for the second goal, the story is still unfolding. Was I able to give them, through my influence and guidance, the skills and self-esteem to reach their unlimited potential? I can only hope that, in trying to be good enough, I have done my part in helping them to succeed in their lives.

My prayer for all parents is that our words, our actions, and the modeling of our own lives will be sufficient to enable our children to go forth and become what and who they want to be. For children I pray that the lives they carve out bring them joy, fulfillment, and a sense of achievement. For all of us, I hope that our influence as parents will inspire our children to do even better with the generations to come. That is the responsibility, the challenge, the excitement, and the satisfaction of parenthood.

by Carol Stern and Andrea Stern Himoff

A S GROWN ADULTS, we realize how lucky we are to say that all our lives, our mom has been our best friend. Not the kind of best friend you meet on the playground swinging from the monkey bars, or the best friend you always sit next to on the bus to and from out-of-town soccer games, or the kind you giggle with in high school geometry class when a cute boy makes a joke. And definitely not the kind who ditches you in seventh grade because you're suddenly not cool enough, or gossips about you behind your back, or offers you your first drink. Our mom has always been a real friend—our confidante, our mentor, our rock. She was a friend we trusted, respected, and listened to because she always trusted, respected, and listened to us. In fact, she was better than any of our other friends because she never betrayed us, made fun of us, or gave us lousy advice. She was our biggest fan. When we were kids, she used to say, "If *I* were eight years old, I would want to be *your* best friend." And she meant it.

Did we always listen to her? No. Did we always tell her everything? Of course not! After all, she was still our *mom*—the person who cared for us, protected us, witnessed every awkward moment of growing up with us, and when she needed to, disciplined us. Still, our mom somehow mastered that great dilemma that most parents face today: how to balance being a parent *and* a friend to her kids. Or maybe, more precisely, how to draw the line between the two.

Our mom did *not* have to be permissive to win our friendship. She didn't have to let us get our way just so we would like her. She didn't have to speak our slang or buy us beer or try to act cool. In fact, she did not have to compromise being our parent at all just to be our friend. She *did* have to be honest with us. She had to spend tons of time with us, do activities with us, and have real conversations with us. She had to earn our trust by always treating us with fairness and respect. Besides giving us her opinions, she also had to hear us out when we disagreed. She sometimes had to put her pride aside and admit when she was wrong, or had to have the humility to learn from us, instead of thinking that we always had to learn from her. She had to confront us when we mistreated her and to apologize when she snapped at us. She had to truly care about us, root for us, compliment and constructively criticize us, understand who we are, and love us for it.

The resulting friendship with our mom was a caliber higher and a layer deeper than any of our other relationships. It was a caliber higher because she brought with her a wealth of knowledge, experience, and mature decision making that we could trust and learn from. It was a layer deeper because she never betrayed or abandoned us. She was there for the long haul, and we knew we had a lifelong bond of love and loyalty that no other friend could beat.

Because of the bond we had, we didn't want to risk losing our friendship by lying to our mom or disobeying her. We knew she was the ultimate authority, and because we respected her and trusted her, we *wanted* to obey her—and usually did. Whenever we didn't, the horrible consequence—worse than any form of punishment—was the knowledge that we had disappointed our mother. The last thing we ever wanted was to put a wedge between us.

As we grew up, we realized our relationship with our mom wasn't like the relationships our friends had with their parents. When we were little, our mom laughed with us, cuddled with us, played with us, and talked to us about everything we were interested in—just like most parents do. As we grew older and made the huge transition from childhood into adolescence, our mom didn't shy away from us like other parents did with their teens. She was comfortable talking with us about the new, grown-up things we were curious about and wanted to know. She didn't seem intimidated by the changes in us. She just stuck with us, and our friendship grew even deeper.

From the time we were teenagers—and especially now, in our adulthood—our friends have always envied the way we could talk openly with our mom about anything at all. Some of their parents let them do anything they wanted as long as the parents didn't have to know about it, but our friends *really* wanted to be able to talk about what they were doing. Today, they wish they could have the kind of openness, support, and thoughtful conversations they witness us having with Mom about men, situations at work, or problems with a friend. Some have even formed friendships with *our* mom because they could not form friendships with their own parents. We feel sad about how much these friends missed by not having a parent who is also a friend.

We believe that the relationship we have with our mother is the single greatest gift we've ever been given—a gift that has taught us the value of respect, showed us how to communicate and build relationships with others, filled us with self-confidence, and essentially shaped us into who we are today. It is the single most important gift we hope to pass down to our own children one day, because we know from experience how powerful and invaluable it is for children to have a strong relationship with their parent or parents.

We hope you'll be inspired by the message of this book so that your children will also reap the enormous benefits of having parents or a parent they want to talk to and listen to most.

ABOUT THE AUTHOR

(CAROL, JOANNE, AND ANDREA)

JOANNE STERN has been a psychotherapist for more than twenty years and a parent for thirty-three, including five years as a single mom. A much-sought-after speaker and keynote presenter, she is an expert in the field of family relationships and communication. She has worked with families and their children and taught parenting courses. Dr. Stern holds a bachelor's and a master's degree from Northwestern University, a double master's in counseling psychology and theology from Fuller Theological Seminary, and a PhD in human and organizational systems from Fielding Graduate University. Joanne lives in Aspen, Colorado, with her husband, Terry Hale.

TO ACCESS MORE RESOURCES FOR GREAT PARENTING
AND TO FIND OUT WHEN AND WHERE YOU CAN SEE DR. STERN
IN PERSON OR IN THE MEDIA, VISIT HER WEB SITE,
PARENTINGISACONTACTSPORT.COM.